3RD EDITION

CYCLOCROSS

TRAINING + TECHNIQUE

SIMON BURNEY

VELO press

Boulder, Colorado

Credits

Abbiorca Photos, back cover, 10, 84, 90, 94, 208 *(bottom)*

Simon Burney, 83

Chris Milliman, 86

Colnago, 34

Crank Brothers, 47

Joolze Dymond, 7, 32, 49, 52, 76, 79, 87, 92, 146, 163, 208 *(top)*

Jason Elhardt, 181

Dan Ellmore, 44

Getty Images, 2, 96, 113

Giant, 29

Larry Hickmott, 12, 168

Don Karle, 69, 71, 73, 74, 80, 82

Jonathan McElvery, cover, 77

John Pierce / Photosport International, 3

John St. Leger, 37

Cor Vos Photography, 59, 75, 142, 149, 166, 179, 185

Graham Watson, 187

Special Thanks to
Tim Johnson
Brian Hludzinski and Boulder Racing
Alan Hills

1830 55th Street
Boulder, Colorado 80301-2700 USA
303/440-0601 · Fax 303/444-6788 · E-mail velopress@competitorgroup.com

Third Edition

Cover design by Jason Farrell
Interior design by BackStory Design

Distributed in the United States and Canada by Ingram Publisher Services

Cataloging-in-Publication Data for this book is available from the Library of Congress

For information on purchasing VeloPress books, please call 800/811-4210, ext. 2169, or visit www.velopress.com.

This book is printed on 100 percent recovered/recycled fiber, 30 percent post-consumer waste, elemental chlorine free, using soy-based inks.

10 11 12 / 10 9 8 7 6 5 4

CONTENTS

FOREWORD

The first cyclocross race I helped promote was the 1995 U.S. 'cross nationals. The nationals back then paled in comparison with our latest production, which recently boasted 2,300 entrants, three days of racing, and a bitchin' beer garden. In the dark old days of 'cross, even the supposedly prestigious nationals tended to be more like a stranding than an event. In 1995 we organized the whole thing in one day. I think we may have gotten 500 entries. We had no snow fencing, no hard fencing, no truss, and about, say, nine banners total. We created a podium stage by planking out a spot on a jungle gym (from which Dick Ring's entire sound system tumbled during the women's race).

Before dawn on race day, snow swirled on the Massachusetts Turnpike as we chugged up to Leicester, a little town foolish enough to let us use its high school grounds, perched atop the Worcester Highlands. Facing a winter storm, the dawn sun simply chose to go back to bed, pulling a blanket of gray clouds back over its head. From the northwest came a savage New England winter storm that flicked the banners and snapped the course tape, advising us, too, to go back to bed. Still, I struggled with Lyle Fulkerson, Tom Stevens, and a ragged band of bike nuts to build the course in worsening conditions.

Meanwhile, all over New England that morning, alarm clocks went off. People peered out of windows to see snowflakes the size of silver dollars burying their cars, coating their walkways and streets. Most of those folks rolled back beneath the blankets, too. But few could fall back to sleep. Eyes blinking, they collectively thought, "They're going to race . . .

they're still going to race . . . they're going to race for the national championships in that stuff."

And they threw off the blankets and grabbed boots, coats, cowbells, hats, and gloves. By the time the elite men started, 12 inches of snow had dumped on the course, and thousands of people had showed up to watch. Cars were crashed and wallets lost; wildly skidding racers smacked into spectators; there were as many wipeouts in the audience as there were in the race.

That's when I realized 'cross could be big in America.

Promoting that event led to a blessed—albeit accidental—career for me as a race announcer, which would mean calling eleven of the next thirteen 'cross nationals, all of the Super Cup series, several regional events, and most recently the U.S. Gran Prix of Cyclocross. I've called countless other races, too—road races, crits, off-road, track, downhill, dual slalom, mountain cross, and so on—but cyclocross has consistently proven the most exciting fodder for my work as an announcer.

Cyclocross isn't like any other form of bike racing. To watch a conventional bicycle stage race is to watch a python eat a pig; there is a tussle, followed by a steady strangulation of the opponent. Typically, the strongest person wins by playing a lot of defense. In 'cross, though, the strongest rider doesn't always win. A 'cross racer has to be the most complete bike racer, holding high cards in all four suits: strength, speed, agility, and brains. The advantage changes depending on the course, the conditions, and how the race unfolds. And on any given day, any number of riders can at least land a punch or two, if not score the win.

Good cyclocross races—good because of the course design, the brevity of the event, and the proximity of spectators—often boil down to boxing matches with mythological impact. You have David taking on Goliath, the wily veteran fending off the anxious rookie, the local hero or heroine up against the out-of-town pro, the lone wolf fighting a pack of goons. Every Sunday in the fall we find Oil Can Harry and

Mighty Mouse, Darth Vader and Luke Skywalker, Milan High against Muncie Central. And anything can happen. One puncture and the pre-race favorite becomes the underdog; one crash at the front and a mid-pack journeyman is thrust into the lead. These races leave us breathless as spectators and hoarse as announcers.

The beauty of cyclocross is that the spectators are as important as the racers. You need not even have a bike to be into 'cross (you should, however, have a good pair of boots). A fully prepared 'cross fanatic comes to the races equipped with bells, wool, body paint, big flags, rain pants, beer, hats, horns, and really, really, really processed meats. It's wonderful.

The fans' role is big partly because they can see nearly the entire race, partly because the courses are so narrow they can touch the riders, partly because they can spill cold beer and hot chili right onto the rider. With bells, horns, and sheer enthusiasm, the fanatics can blow life back into a dead man. It's so easy to quit a mountain bike race or a road race or a crit. But in 'cross your surrender will have witnesses.

I grew up watching and playing all sorts of sports. Later I competed in and announced at all sorts of bike races. But at the Super Cup finals in San Francisco's Presidio in 1999—the most exciting bike race I've ever watched—I experienced something of a harmonic convergence among announcers, spectators, and riders that never happens in other sports.

The race had boiled down to a five-rider fight. Three well-paid Saturn pros—the McCormack brothers, Frank and Mark, along with their henchman, Bart Bowen—had to fend off two challengers. One of these was the young phenom Tim Johnson, then riding for CCB. The other was the raging bull, Marc Gullickson, a day after he had restored his broken career by riding solo to a national title.

These five riders went at it hammer and tongs for fifty minutes. Everybody had landed blows; everybody had been put on the canvas only to fight back to the leaders. The popular "Gully" had been dropped several times. But each time he clawed his way back to the lead group and clung to their wheels in desperation.

On the final run-up, Gully launched a counterattack that only Popeye could match in a cartoon. He sprang away from the powerful and mighty Saturn boys like a deer. Johnson could not respond. The crowd—in the thousands—reacted with a roar I've never heard since. I barked out the call so hard my spleen nearly burst.

Here was a rider punching back against all odds, refusing to surrender to the younger, the stronger, and the better-funded opponents. He landed a blow against the boss, the phone company, the motor vehicle registry, credit card companies, and all the evil forces of the world that keep virtuous people down. This was more than 'cross: this was Chamberlain at Gettysburg, Leonidas at Thermopylae, Chard at Rorke's Drift. And in that minute Gully looked like he would win the day and the series. But with just 600 meters to go in the entire U.S. season, the McCormacks and Bowen and Johnson all remounted their bikes and made a gritty charge after Gullickson. The place went bananas.

At that moment I turned to see a professorial, bearded man in corduroy gazing at Gully's attack. In a curious spasm, he jumped about, rang a bell violently, and belted out a visceral howl trapped way too long inside his body. This man's bespectacled face was wet with tears! Crying, laughing, screaming for a working-class hero . . . 'cross had effected a primal rolfing of his soul.

This is as good as sport—and I mean any sport in this world—can ever get.

Welcome to cyclocross. Read on.

Richard Fries
Boston, 2007

'CROSSWORD

Being a bookish sort, I scored myself a copy of Simon Burney's original hardback edition of *Cyclocross* long before I ever bought an actual cyclocross bike, reasoning that a guy doesn't join a congregation without reading its bible.

Like many neo-'crossers in the late 1980s, I did my first race on a mountain bike, then had a frame-building friend add cantilever bosses to a Specialized Sirrus road frame to get more of the actual feel of the discipline. I soon made the leap to an actual 'cross frame, a canary yellow Pinarello, which 16-some-odd years later leans against a wall in my garage with a cracked down tube. Three functional machines—two Steelman Eurocrosses and a Soma Fabrications Double Cross—hang from the ceiling, ready to ride. A Voodoo Wazoo and most of the parts needed to make it roll are in there, too.

I blame Simon for this extravagance. His book was comprehensive but entirely without pedantry. Indeed, it was a fun read, and what I learned from it brought me some modest success on the Colorado masters circuit during the late 1990s while I lavished a few hundred thousand dollars on the bicycle industry that I otherwise would have wasted on health care, vacations, or jewelry for the wife (instead, I bought her a 'cross bike).

Subsequent editions have been equally valuable, and I'm sure I've helped shift a copy or two for VeloPress, because every time someone tells me, "You know, I've been thinking about getting into cyclocross this fall," I reply, "Buy Simon Burney's book." And mind you, I don't even get a commission. Greater love hath no man, as the saying goes. I could really use the money, too, because Mark Nobilette is welding me up a custom 'cross frame even as we speak.

Does anyone out there know of a good 12-step program for cyclocrossaholics? Maybe it's in this edition. Send up a flare if you stumble across anything. I'll be running up a hill somewhere, wearing a perfectly rideable bike.

Patrick O'Grady
Mad Dog Media, 2007

Introduction

Since the publication of the first edition of *Cyclocross* in 1990, the world of 'cross has moved on significantly. New rules have been introduced reducing the amount of time riders spend off their bikes, and the circuits that races are run on have evolved accordingly. The bikes themselves, although mostly the same in appearance, have undergone transformations as technology has advanced. Women's racing has finally been embraced, as has the under-23 (U23) men's category, and both now have a World Cup series. And although the hub of 'cross remains in central Europe—in recent times the sport has been largely the domain of the Belgians—the growth of cyclocross in the United States has been amazing to watch. Maybe it's a result of the "Lance effect" on cycling in general, since legendary Tour de France winner Lance Armstrong is probably solely responsible for putting more people on bikes than any other cyclist, opening up a whole new arena of sport to Americans. Or maybe the large growth spurt is just part of the quirky nature of a discipline that has never quite fit into mainstream cycling—"the ugly redheaded stepchild of cycling," as one journalist lovingly described it!

Whatever the reason for its growth, cyclocross is special, and once you've had a taste of it you are very likely to be hooked. As any dedicated cyclocross racer knows, when that happens your life will never be quite the same again. Your washing machine will need replacing on a regular basis because sand, grass, and grit will clog up the works, your shoes will

The crowds may have gotten bigger, the course marking more substantial, and of course now you have to wear a helmet, but even sixty years ago the objective was the same: Get yourself and your machine around the course as quickly as possible.

never be quite dry, your bike-carrying shoulder will be bruised every September, and you will dream of a Christmas vacation in Flanders to see how it's really, and I mean really, done.

What Is Cyclocross?

Time for a short history lesson. Back in the day, there was a French army private by the name of Daniel Gousseau who used to accompany his horse-riding general around the French forests on his bike. He enjoyed this so much that he started inviting his friends along, and as we all know, when friends get together the competitive juices start flowing. Once they figured out how they could beat the horse, they started racing each other around the woods, and lo and behold, cyclocross racing had been invented.

Now this was early on in the 1900s, and for a while, this style of cycling remained an underground activity practiced by just a few cyclists in disjointed areas of France, but as the word spread, races became more abundant and organized. The first French national championship competition—organized by Gousseau—was in 1902. In 1910, Tour de France winner Octave Lapize credited his Tour win to his off-season racing off-road, and it suddenly became useful as well as fun to race 'cross. The Tour connection continued at the first-ever cyclocross World Championships held in Paris in 1950, won by 1947 Tour de France winner Jean Robic. And in 2004, Lance Armstrong raced a bit of 'cross to keep himself occupied during the off-season, causing a few others to check out the 'cross scene.

History lesson over!

On any given weekend in Europe and increasingly in North America, the crowds come out to watch the spectacle. This particular crowd takes advantage of a holiday on December 26 by watching a World Cup race at Hofstade, Belgium.

So that's how it started, but what exactly is it all about? Cyclocross is a winter cycling discipline raced over a season that starts in early September and culminates in the middle of February. It takes place predominantly off-road, and according to the rules laid out by the Union Cycliste Internationale (UCI, International Cycling Union), the world governing body for cycling, "a cyclo-cross course shall include road, country and forest paths and meadowland alternating in such a way as to ensure changes in the pace of the race and allowing riders to recuperate after difficult sections." Circuits must be between 2.5 and 3.5 kilometers long. That means that a cyclocross circuit can be set up just about anywhere, as long as the location has enough varied terrain and enough space to fit the regulations.

Circuits vary tremendously from place to place, but all comprise features and terrain calling for bike-handling skills, strength, and speed. In addition, every cyclocross course includes sections that are unrideable, forcing the riders to dismount and run with their bikes. Although the rules state that at least 90 percent of the course must be rideable, that still gives spectators a possible 250 meters in which to cheer on and occasionally ridicule their running or staggering favorites.

Although race distances vary depending on the terrain, race duration is standard: 30 minutes for juveniles (12–15 years); 40 minutes for juniors (16–18 years) and women; 50 minutes for U23s (19–22 years), if they have a separate race; and 60 minutes for seniors (over 18).

All racing is controlled by the national cycling federation of the particular country under the rules of the UCI, and it's the UCI that takes care of the sharp end of the sport: the World Cup and the World Championships.

The racing season lasts for about twenty-five weeks from September through February, with races occurring on weekends or midweek holidays, but the number of races varies widely from one country to the next. In Great Britain, for example, there were 168 races during the 2006–2007 season, but most of these were small, local events ideal for first-timers and people looking for a training session. Out of this 168, only 6 races qualified for the UCI calendar, a compilation of races all over the world governed by UCI rules and meeting certain standards. These races must carry a minimum prize list but in return are granted points toward the UCI world ranking. Compare that with the United States, where the number of UCI races is much larger and growing rapidly. There were 28 U.S. races on the UCI calendar in the 2006–2007 season, and close to 40 listed for the 2007–2008 season. Even a small nation can generate a great deal of interest in this discipline.

As you'll remember from your short history lesson, the sport started out primarily as a way for the road riders of the time to stay in shape and have some competitive fun during their winter "off-season," and for a number of riders this is still the case. But over time, and especially since the first World Championships in Paris in 1950, 'cross has developed into a sport in its own right. It became necessary to split the championships into amateur and professional events in 1967, and this is how it remained until 1995, when the whole of cycle sport became "open" and open elite championship competitions were held, with a supporting U23 race for the younger riders. The U23 race was a European Championship in its first year but was granted full World Championship status in 1996. Although junior men's World Championships have always been held to support the open and U23 categories, it took until 2000 for a women's race to be added by the UCI, and now, in line with the road and mountain-bike calendars, there is also a women's season-long World Cup competition. This competition, along with the guys' competition, lost its separate overall classification in 2006 but became integrated into the UCI world ranking instead.

Today cyclocross is a major spectator sport in countries such as Belgium and Holland, and although soccer still reigns supreme, 'cross is best-of-the-rest as far as a wintertime spectator sport goes. Along with consistently large paying crowds of 10,000 or more at the events, television covers all the big races; two Belgian channels, VRT and Kanaal 2, cover the majority of World Cup, Super Prestige, and GVA series races (the GVA is named for *Gazette Van Antwerpen,* a national daily newspaper), and a large proportion of them are shown live. For a small country, viewing rates are high. The stations report viewing figures of 500,000 for the popular Super Prestige races; at the 2006 Worlds in Zeddam, Holland, VRT had over 1 million people watching, and a record 1.25 million (plus 36,000 paying spectators) saw Erwin Vervecken cross the line after his battle with Jonathan Page at the Hooglede-Gits Worlds in the Flemish heartland in 2007. With the daily newspapers covering every detail of the riders and the races, sponsors are encouraged to support events, teams, and riders, and the fans have an in-depth knowledge of the sport and its stars.

These stars are the draw, and they are household names. They are also relatively well paid. Riders are retained by teams and paid a salary, and in addition they receive start money—either a sum prearranged through an agent to show up and start the race, if it is outside of the World Cup, or a fee laid out according to World Cup rules based on the rider's current world ranking. UCI-status races are posted on domestic calendars, and riders often schedule their season to chase points and increase their start money. Prize money rewards the successful, and a combination of salary, start and prize monies, and revenue from endorsement contracts signed on an individual basis provides a good living for the champions, though their contemporaries on the road and other elite athletes in more mainstream sports can earn more. Some of the races also pay start money to some of the leading road riders to help draw the crowds. In these cases, the road rider gets a nice workout plus some pocket money, the race promoter gets a bigger crowd and a useful "hook" for television, and the crowds get to see their favorite road star "up close and personal."

Most countries cannot boast this level of popularity for the sport and probably never will, but there is no telling just where cyclocross might begin to generate greater interest in the coming years. Switzer-

After an early season spoiled by injury, Jonathan Page came back strongly in 2007 to become the first American male to stand on an Elite World Championship podium with a superb second place behind Erwin Vervecken of Belgium.

land was the place to race back in the 1980s when the first edition of this book came out, and there is no reason to think that the United States could not be that place in the next few years; after all, ten years ago the sport was still in its infancy in America, but now the country is on a roll, with big participation numbers and a high level of ability at the front of European and World Championship races. If a proposed World Cup can make the UCI calendar in 2008, it's not infeasible to imagine an American World Championship within a few years.

For the serious rider, the ultimate aim is to become a champion. But there are races and competitions in cyclocross at every level—local, national, and international. Regular cyclocross training and events give summer road riders and mountain-bike racers the chance to prepare for their season and improve their fitness and bike-handling skills at whatever level they choose.

In general, cycling has become a twelve-month-a-year occupation. No longer do summertime racers take long rests during the winter months; nor do 'cross riders rest in the summer. By taking part in each other's events, both types of riders are finding that they can hone their abilities and improve their fitness generally. But if serious competition is not your scene, that is no reason to avoid 'cross. It is a sport that can be ridden at any level and one that provides an enormous amount of fun and self-fulfillment.

Cyclocross for the Roadie

For a number of reasons, cyclocross can be an ideal winter activity for the summer road racer. As an aid to improved bike handling it cannot be beaten: After a winter riding 'cross, bad road surfaces, racing in the rain, and descending will be a lot easier to cope with, as 'cross teaches you how to race and handle your bike well in all conditions.

Given the amount of effort required in a 'cross race—not to compete at a high level but just simply to get around the course—if you're a road racer there is no better way to supplement your winter training than by taking part in occasional competitive outings off-road. 'Cross requires great strength, agility, and cardiovascular fitness, and these are all qualities that road riders try to develop during the winter months.

Long, steady distance work on the road bike, regular "crosstraining" such as stretching and running, and core and circuit training are all essential and should be continued, but 'cross can add the competitive element to keep you going.

If the weather is bad for long periods, it sometimes becomes dangerous to go out on the roads, and very uncomfortable in cold weather. But an hour's 'cross can give you a workout similar to a two- or three-hour road ride—plus it allows you to avoid the icy roads, keep warm, and still get in a high-quality training session.

Continental road riders have always used 'cross more than their British or American counterparts, even at the very highest levels. One of the all-time greats, Bernard Hinault, was a real fan of 'cross and used it regularly as part of his winter preparation. He claimed that it provided riders with complementary training and taught them to improvise, as they never knew what surface they would have to ride on. For those of you too young to remember some old guy called Hinault, look no further than Chris Horner, an American, or Roger Hammond, who is British, to see two English speakers who are paid to perform on the road, but who appreciate the payoff they receive from their participation in 'cross racing. A cyclocross race anywhere in Europe will always attract a good turn-out of road riders, and while it is true that many of the stars are paid good money to show up because they attract big crowds, they are still there for a purpose—to prepare for the summer.

If you doubt the value of replacing your traditional Sunday training ride with a cyclocross race, then race the smaller Saturday races instead. They are usually low-key affairs, and this will leave your Sunday free for your normal training on the road. And don't just *race* on the 'cross course; it is well worth putting aside one day a week to train on it, too. You can often find some organized 'cross training going on one evening a week somewhere close by. Don't worry about doing the interval training that the specialists use; just try going for a one-hour ride and use the session as a guide to your fitness—I'll bet it makes you gasp.

After a full summer road season on the ProTour circuit, the legendary American Chris Horner can still see the sense in competing in cyclocross during the winter.

Assuming you have ridden a full road summer season through to September, there are two possible lines of attack for a 'cross season. The first option is to go straight into the 'cross season as soon as it starts, while you still have good form from the road, take a break in early November, and come back to it at the end of the month. The second option is to take a break from racing in October, start riding 'cross in November, and then race straight through February. Both options will give you a good break from competitive cycling and prevent any staleness from creeping in. You should continue doing your usual winter work, and continue riding through to at least the middle of

> ## CYCLOCROSS ADVANTAGE
>
> If there is a particular weakness in your road cycling—for example, perhaps you cannot corner at high speeds or sprint as well as you'd like, or you're not coping with bad weather or super-high intensities as you know you could—a season of cyclocross is exactly what you need.
>
> Cyclocross racing is a lot like criterium racing, only tougher. 'Cross courses have pavement, grass, sand, mud, off-cambers, steep climbs, fast descents, hairpin turns, and more. Being able to conquer these elements at an extremely high intensity helps me to be better prepared for racing a criterium or road race, both of which are typically held on paved courses that are free of debris and quite predictable. Cornering at 35 miles per hour in a pack of road cyclists will seem relaxing compared to an off-camber descent on muddy terrain. Also, the changes in speed during a road race or criterium are likely to be more manageable after repeatedly accelerating from a near standstill back up to full speed during multiple laps of a cyclocross race.
>
> **MARK McCORMACK**

January, depending on the race calendar in your region. This gives you February and March to get used to the longer distances required for the road, but with some quality sessions already "in the bank."

Cyclocross for the Mountain-Bike Racer

When mountain bikes first came onto the scene and the World Cup was in its infancy, in the early to mid-1990s, mountain biking was largely dominated by Euro 'cross riders who had made the transition. For the likes of Thomas Frischknecht, Henrik Djernis, David Baker, and Daniele Pontoni, 'cross was all they ever knew. In the new millennium,

Roger Hammond became junior world 'cross champion in 1992 and in the fifteen subsequent years has become a highly respected road rider with a passion and talent for the spring classics in Belgium. His preparation for the Classics still includes a few weeks of cyclocross from late November to the British championships in early January, as can be seen here with yet another win in Discovery colors in 2006.

the crossover of expertise gradually lessened, and now very few of the top 'cross riders race mountain bikes, or vice versa. Sure, there are exceptions to the rule—Thomas Frischknecht is probably the one cyclist who can be competitive at both disciplines and who still occasionally races in the winter, and more recently Sven Nys has been dabbling with mountain-bike racing to see whether he can make the grade and win a medal at the 2008 Beijing Olympics—but they are rare. From the top ten in the 2006 'Cross Worlds, only Nys has been seen on a mountain bike, and from the top ten in the 2006 Mountain Bike Worlds, only Frischknecht and Britain's Liam Killeen ride more than occasional races in the winter. Killeen was in fact narrowly beaten in a sprint finish at the 2006 British National Championships by road star Roger Hammond—proof, if any were needed, that class shines through irrespective of which discipline a rider competes in. In the United States, Ryan Trebon is the 2006–2007 national champ at both disciplines, but his focus is turning more toward 'cross, and it is increasingly unlikely that he would figure at the front of a mountain-bike World Championship.

It is certainly becoming increasingly unlikely that we would see a world-class mountain biker take top honors at the 'cross Worlds, and with the exception of Nys, the same can be said of 'cross specialists taking the game to the elite mountain-bike competitors, but that's no reason not to try racing in the winter if you come from a mountain-bike background.

Cyclocross can give mountain-bike racers an edge to their performance. This edge comes mainly from the added bike-handling skills required, the extra speed, plus the extra fitness gained from training eleven months of the year instead of just seven. The other benefits are in line with those gained by road riders.

In many countries, it is possible to race the smaller 'cross races on a mountain bike, and initially this is fine, as it reduces the outlay of expense for extra machinery. But the real advantage will come from racing a 'cross bike during the winter, and then switching to a mountain

BIKE-HANDLING SKILLS AND FITNESS

Whether you are a roadie, a mountain biker, or a triathlete, racing cyclocross or simply riding a 'cross bike to mix up your training is a great way to hone your technical riding skills and raise your fitness level.

A cyclocross bike is essentially a road bike with a little extra tread on the wheels, so if you can maneuver your bike quickly and easily through mud, sand, grass, and dirt, just imagine what you can do on pavement. Road racers who compete in 'cross are some of the best bike handlers in the peloton. As a mountain-bike racer, my training buddies and I would ride some of our favorite trails on our cyclocross bikes just to change things up and work on our technical skills. After riding a 'cross bike on tight and twisty singletrack for a while, you'll be amazed how easy it feels to be on a mountain bike with suspension. And, as far as fitness goes, I don't think you can push your body harder than you can in cyclocross. It's an hour of lung-busting effort that will surely raise your lactate threshold, not to mention your tolerance for pain.

BRANDON DWIGHT

bike in the summer. On a "proper" 'cross course, a 'cross bike should be the faster option, both for riding and for carrying. This increased speed develops new skills and faster reflexes that can be transferred to the mountain bike when spring rolls around.

Gaining experience on a 'cross bike holds great benefits for mountain bikers. The main improvements you will see come summertime are a faster race start; greater confidence when racing in close quarters with other competitors; improved skill in dismounting for obstacles, in covering unrideable sections on foot with the bike shouldered, and in remounting afterward; and an ability to stay more relaxed and in better control at faster speeds on a variety of surfaces.

CHAPTER 1

Getting Started

A bike, a helmet, and a license are all you need to race, and there are plenty of successful racers who started their careers with nothing more than that. It helps, though, to have some guidance.

Getting involved with a cycling club that already has members competing is a good first step to take on your way to racing 'cross. It is possible to go it alone and join your national federation as an individual, but in a club or team you will be exposed to good advice and gain other benefits that will help speed your progress. If you can find a club or team in your local area that has an interest in 'cross, then so much the better; perhaps it already promotes a race or has a team who travels together to races. Whatever the case, if you can get involved with somebody who knows about 'cross, it will save you a lot of the time you would otherwise spend learning the ropes and organizing everything on your own. If you are unsure how to find a club, contact your national cycling federation, which can provide you with a list of clubs in your area. Failing that, try your local bike shop; the owners or employees of reasonably good shops usually know what is going on locally.

If you intend to compete in any large races or hope to compete abroad, you will need a racing license. The license you need is the same as the one that is required for road racing, so if you are already competing, you should have one. If not, get one—then you can race during the summer as well as the winter.

Next on the list: Find out about the races held in your area. Knowing which races you may enter can help you set personal goals, and in some cases it is necessary to sign up early. Again, try the club or the bike shop; the latter may have posters or flyers advertising forthcoming events. The Internet is also a good source of information about races. With a quick search, you can locate calendars and race programs for your area. Local and national cycling magazines may also list upcoming events. National federations usually issue a complete calendar at the beginning of the winter season. In the United Kingdom, this comes in the form of a handbook that lists not only the races but also all the rules and regulations of racing, along with other useful information. The same is always available on federation Web sites.

Be sure to check the deadlines for entering. Not all races offer raceday registration; some, especially at the higher levels, require participants to send in their registration up to three weeks in advance. If you can't register online, you can usually download entry forms to fill out and mail in.

Converting a Bike for Cyclocross

ROAD BIKES

Let's assume you have joined a club and you know where the races are; let's say you even have a helmet—and it better be a good one (see "Headgear and Eyewear" section in Chapter 2). All you're missing is a suitable bike. In all likelihood, you will not have a specially built 'cross machine just yet. If you do, then read no further. But to be honest, until you have tried the sport and decided that you like it and want to continue, you are probably better off adapting an old road bike—maybe your training or winter bike—than you are buying more specialized equipment.

So what are the differences between a road bike and a 'cross bike? At a glance they may seem very similar; they have the same frame shape, the same wheel size, and the same dropped handlebars and general overall appearance. But look a little harder and you will find some significant differences. Although the frame is the same shape, some of the dimensions are different. A cyclocross bike has more space between the wheels and the frame to accommodate fatter tires than those you would use on the road and to allow the wheels to keep turning in particularly muddy conditions. This becomes apparent if you look at the spaces between the front wheel and the top of the forks, between the back wheel and the back of the seat tube, and between the sides of the back wheel and the inside of the chainstays on a 'cross bike. You will see more room for the mud to escape.

At the same time, you will notice that the brakes are not the standard caliper type you have on your road bike; instead, they are cantilever-style brakes that bolt onto pivots attached to the front forks and the rear seat stays. The main reason for using this style of braking system is that the simplicity of its design provides that all-important mud clearance. Cantilever brakes used to be significantly more powerful than regular caliper brakes; nowadays, a good caliper system is just as powerful. But caliper brakes have more modulation, so that on the road you can control braking by degrees; a cantilever brake on the road tends to grab. Fine braking and control are harder to achieve with cantilever brakes, but this is less of an issue off-road.

So that's the frame, but there are other differences. The wheels on your road bike, for instance, will be the same size (diameter) as a 'cross bike wheel but will have narrower, smoother tires on them. For riding off-road you need a fatter tire to absorb the shock and give you more contact with the ground, and you also need grip. That is why on a 'cross bike you will see tires with a pattern of knobs or arrows, which bite into the surface you are riding on and reduce the amount of time you spend sliding around. Finally, the gearing on a 'cross bike is generally lower than on a road bike to allow you to continue pedaling at slower speeds. In cyclocross, you don't need those hard gears that you use only occasionally even on your road bike—the ones you might use on those rare days when you have the opportunity to fly along a nicely surfaced, gradual downhill road with a tailwind. Lower gearing in practice means a smaller number of teeth on the front chainrings and more teeth on the sprockets on the rear wheel, compared to a road bike, so it's not something most people would notice at first glance, but it's nevertheless an important feature on a 'cross bike. And that's pretty much it—small, sometimes unnoticeable differences in equipment and design that don't change the look of a bike significantly, but certainly make each bike more specialized for the type of riding it is designed for. A cyclocross bike is, simply put, easier to ride and race off-road.

With a standard road bike, there are a few modifications you can perform to make your life off-road a little easier. But with standard road-frame clearances, you are going to be very limited in what you can do about problems caused by mud clogging everything up on bad-weather days. Only a change of frame can solve that problem.

The first thing to improve is traction. Good traction is relatively easy to achieve by fitting 'cross tires with plenty of grip. If your wheels are fitted with rims for tubulars (sew-ups), then the choices of relatively cheap rubber are not vast, but you should be able to find some 'cross tubulars online if your local shop doesn't stock them. If you have clincher tires, then the range of choices will be broader and different options will be easier to find. If you are confused by the choices, just make sure you get a size (width) that will fit into your frame and give you as much grip as possible. A 30-millimeter tire should fit; most brands offer a "dry" and a "mud" option, so go for the "mud." These tires will suffice for any conditions you should encounter, and at this stage there is no need to change tires for different course conditions.

You will need lower gears to cope with the slower speeds, harder terrain, and other obstacles common to 'cross. Assuming you have a double crankset, the best and cheapest way to make the alteration is to simply change the cluster of cogs on the back wheel. Most standard cranksets come fitted with 39/53 chainrings, or you might be lucky and have a compact crank with something like 34/48. These numbers relate to the number of teeth on the chainrings that are fitted onto the right-hand crank; the lower the number of teeth, the lower the gear (and the easier it is to pedal up a hill). The first number is the size of the inner chainring; the second is the size of the outer chainring. If you have the standard setup with 39/53, leave the big ring on the outside and adjust your front derailleur as close as you can to it to keep your chain on (though you will probably be using only the inner ring for racing initially). If you have the 34/48 setup, then leave it as it is and use both chainrings. For the cogset at the back, use the biggest sprocket your gear system will cope with; in this case, the higher the number of teeth on the cassette, the lower the gear. If you are running Shimano, then it will be a 25 or a 27; if it's Campagnolo, then it's likely to be a 26. Don't forget to check the chain length; better still, fit a new chain. This will give you the wide range of gears you will need, but at first, even with this gearing, anything you cannot ride you will have to run. You will be amazed by how much more you will be able to ride as your fitness and technique improve, so don't worry if at first you seem to be off the bike as much as on it.

The next thing you will have to do is change the pedals. Chances are you have some kind of clipless road setup—Look, Time, Shimano, or something similar—and road shoes to match. You know how slippery these can be just walking out of the house to go on a training ride, so racing 'cross with them would be an adventure, to say the least! If you own a mountain bike, rob the pedals off it and use the matching shoes. Otherwise, invest in a pair of off-road pedals and shoes. Make sure they are double-sided pedals, as the single-sided ones just take too much time to enter.

You will be stuck with the brake calipers you have, as they will be suited to the frame's clearances. But if you are running an economy model, then I advise upgrading the brake pads to something suited to the rims you intend to use. And make sure they are well adjusted— you will need to slow down as effectively as possible in wet and slippery conditions that affect braking distance. In addition, take it easy the first time you are out; you will need to get a feel for the differences in slowing on and off road.

Adjust your position on the bike very slightly from your normal road position to gain better control on rough ground and to help with the initially awkward mounts and dismounts. Lower the saddle very slightly, but by no more than 1 centimeter (about 0.4 in.), and raise the handlebars a similar amount. Next time you retape your handlebars, raise the brake levers a touch to allow yourself to be in a more upright position, or simply loosen the stem where it clamps the bars and swing them up a couple of centimeters. You will be riding on the brake levers a lot, so make sure you are comfortable.

Once you have replaced your tires and pedals and adjusted your position, your brakes, and your front derailleur, your old bike will be fine to get you started. If you catch the 'cross bug and go for a specially built bike, you can easily return your old bike to its original state, use it for a spare race bike, or make it an extra training machine.

MOUNTAIN BIKES

Even the most committed "roadie" is likely to have a mountain bike hidden away in the depths of the garage, and this is likely to be the machine that comes out when the urge hits to get on the start line of a 'cross. Built for off-road use, the mountain bike has all the basic requirements. And with a few refinements, you can put together a nice, fast bike.

Start with the frame. There isn't a whole lot you can do with this, but take off any surplus accessories, such as bottle cages, reflectors, racks, mini-pump, and the like. If you have suspension front or rear, either lock it out or adjust it to make it as "hard" as possible. If you have the opportunity, you could always replace the fork with a rigid alternative, which would also lighten the bike considerably.

Now turn your attention to the wheels. Fit the narrowest tires you can find; normally, 1.5-inchers are readily available. These will provide a lower rolling resistance and increase the mud clearance. If you have a selection of cogs at your disposal, go with a standard 12–28 instead of 12–32, and drop off the inner ("granny") chainring. You won't need it, and it just adds weight and a place for more crud to accumulate.

The rest of the bike can pretty much stay as is. You could add a set of dropped bars, but this is a major ordeal—to do this would mean a new stem, bar, brake lever/shifters, and a change in riding position. It may be best to leave the bike with straight bars for now and replace them later, or wait, save up for a 'cross frame, transfer some components, and use dropped bars on that.

One quick word of warning: If you intend to compete in any races on the UCI calendar, you will not be allowed to start on a mountain bike (or a 'cross bike with disc brakes, for that matter). For small, local events, a converted mountain bike should not be a problem, but it may be best to check with the organizer before you show up.

Acquiring a Coach

One of the best steps you can take as a young rider, or even as a more experienced rider new to 'cross, is to get a good coach. A coach can help you learn new techniques effectively, teach you how to train specifically for 'cross, and help you design a training schedule. You will also find it enormously beneficial just to have someone to talk to who knows the sport.

Your coach does not have to have been a top rider, though obviously some race experience is handy. There are even top coaches around who have never raced but nonetheless have the ability to communicate and get the best out of riders. Find someone you respect and who will listen to any thoughts, feelings, or worries you may have that could impact your cycling; you must be able to trust your coach implicitly to get the most out of the training.

Most federations have lists of coaches, and nowadays coaching is a bigger business than it was a decade ago, so look for ads in magazines and on Web sites. But specialist 'cross coaches are a rare breed, so it may take some time to find the right person. Maybe your national federation has a coaching department or a 'cross department that can provide information. Cyclocross coaching certification programs are in operation in some countries, and someone with this qualification will be the best person to approach. Many 'cross coaches are already qualified as road or track coaches, too, which is a bonus. It is best if you can find someone in your local area to meet with in person on a regular basis, because then the coach can observe your riding style and suggest techniques, but Internet coaching with some phone time is also a good option. Talk to as many people as you can, and find someone you can get along with easily. When you find the right person, you will know.

Season Planning

As a rule, the 'cross season runs from early September to mid-February, with races every weekend. The major races are usually at about the same time each year, and the national and World Championship dates are fixed by the UCI.

Internationally, the World Cup season gets under way in early October, around the same time as the main opening race or national series event in each country. By the end of October and into November, things are heating up, the road season is long gone, and just about everyone intending to race has started his or her season. For Europeans, a glut of racing in the holiday season sees riders trying to reach top form for the second weekend in January at their national championships, which for most countries also serve as the World Championship selection race. The United States, however, holds its nationals in early December, which can make the U.S. season a short, intense affair. This schedule gives the leading Americans an opportunity to travel to Europe to race over the Christmas holiday period, when races are held every day, and some stay for the Worlds. The World Cup final round comes in mid-January, usually the weekend before the World Championship, which is either the last weekend in January or first weekend in February. After that, only a couple of weekends of racing remain for showing off the new rainbow jersey— or exacting revenge on the person wearing it!

Between all the major dates, small races and series abound, and these are the ones that you should enter as a beginner. A lot of smaller races are held on Saturdays, giving the regular 'cross riders a good warm-up for the major races, which are on Sundays. They also give road riders an excellent training session, leaving Sunday free for a club run or training on the road.

If you are a novice in the sport, you will need to take your commitments to other cycling events into consideration when planning your season. If you are a road or mountain-bike racer, then a September to February season will not be optimal because you will need a break after your summer season; it may make more sense to start your 'cross season in November or early December.

Specializing

There may come a time when you suddenly realize that 'cross is for you and that you would like to concentrate on it as your top sport. As you will see in later chapters, 'cross riders today can compete for ten months a year, and summer racing, whether in road or mountain-bike events, is a vital part of their preparation.

If you are a relative beginner eager to do well at 'cross, you should go straight to a full-year training plan (see Chapter 4). But if you started your cycling life with the summer as your target season, you will have to adapt your usual plan to cater to the different needs of 'cross. If you are used to competing from March to September and then taking five months off, it is a big change to take on two racing seasons in a year. It is vital to have adequate rest and recovery times built into your training schedule to perform well throughout both seasons.

Once you incorporate a 'cross season, you are likely to discover that you can ride as well during the summer as you ever did as a road specialist. There are several reasons for this. You will be fitter for longer stretches of the year, and the level of conditioning you attain by training and racing for longer periods will last throughout both seasons. You will be training more than you are used to, and you will be resting more effectively (if you follow the advice provided in later chapters). Ideally, your training will build in stages followed by rest periods.

Most people who are just riding a summer season tend to train from January 1, start racing around March 1, and finish in July because they are fed up—though "stale" is a better term. Because they are so keen to get started each year, they train hard from the New Year, usually in grim weather, start racing as soon as they can, and never take a break—but even if the body can take it, the mind cannot. So they finish their season early and plan to have a really good crack at the next season; they train really hard all winter long, and then the same thing happens.

Most 'cross specialists, in contrast, will not be racing until April, when the weather is probably better. They'll have a steadier start into the season, and they'll still be enthusiastic well into the summer, reaching a peak in July and August when the big races occur and the weather is nice. The advantages of winter racing rub off during the summer.

One of the biggest changes any racer goes through during the summer is one of attitude. When you know that the road races are merely a stepping-stone to greater things in the winter, it takes a certain amount of pressure off, and it's surprising how many riders end up performing better when there is less pressure.

CHAPTER 2

Equipment

Over the years progress in 'cross bike technology has tended to parallel progress in road bike technology; if a component or frame material or design was found to work well on a road bike, it was a safe bet it would be utilized by a 'cross rider or frame manufacturer the following season, especially if it produced a lighter, stronger, or more efficient 'cross bike.

The days are long gone when riders had to "create" their own 'cross parts—by, for example, adapting road pedals, or removing teeth from chainrings to make chainguards. In those days, independent, specialist engineers would knock out 'cross parts in their spare time. Today, 'cross bikes and equipment are mainstream.

The bicycle industry in general, and frame and component manufacturers in particular, have experienced massive change over the past two decades. The technical revolution started with the arrival of the mountain bike in the 1990s. Within a decade, bike-component design radically altered cycling, changing not so much how a bike looked, but how effectively it worked, how much it weighed, and how fast and comfortable it was to ride.

With a change of brakes and tires and a few other tweaks, the modern 'cross bike could quite easily be a road bike. The tweaks include minor differences in frame geometry and clearance, along with slightly lower gearing. Ninety-five percent of the parts you would use on the road, however, are perfectly suitable for 'cross, which means that 'cross is accessible to everyone, and you don't have to join a secret society to acquire the necessary equipment and learn how to use it.

If you are going to take 'cross seriously, then eventually you are going to have to outlay for two bikes. As a starting point, one will be fine, and you may want to progress to a second bike gradually, perhaps by using a cheaper frame and parts for your second 'cross bike at first. But no doubt at all, to perform to the best of your ability, you will need two identical bikes. The reason, in a word, is mud. The accumulation of mud interferes with components, which means regular changes of machine during a race. Efficient and regular bike changing will become an important part of your game plan—races can be won or lost over the time it takes to click back into a pedal, and if your pedal is clean, you'll be that much more likely to beat the guy whose pedal was clogged coming off the last obstacle.

The following sections cover what to look for when shopping for—or building—the perfect 'cross bike. You will find that in some cases more thought and preparation are required than for a road machine. Fads in equipment come and go, technology is still playing a fast-moving part in what is available, and ideas change. So it's important to keep your eyes open at races and see what's being used, especially among the top people. The number of choices, especially in frames and wheels, is tenfold what it was a few years ago, and more complete off-the-shelf 'cross bikes are now available from the major manufacturers.

A complete 'cross bike for sale in a shop in the 1990s would have been put together by the shop, but now the choices are vast. Only a few years ago, I would have laughed at anyone who told me I would soon be able to pick up a respectable 'cross bike in my local sporting goods superstore, but today I can, and it's an indication of how far the sport has progressed.

Budget 'cross bikes are now easy to find, and most manufacturers
have at least one that is good for beginners.

The Cyclocross Bike

THE FRAME

Once upon a time, it was a simple choice. To get a dedicated 'cross
bike you had to go see your local frame builder to have a custom steel
frame built, or find an Italian "Alan" aluminum frame. The latter had
been around since the late 1970s, and so you knew it would be the
right geometry and have the right specifications for what you wanted;
well, it had to be right, since everyone was using it.

But that was then and this is now, and custom frames are pretty
much a thing of the past. While Alan still makes some cutting-edge
'cross frames, so do a hundred other manufacturers. You'll need to do
some research to find out which type is best for you within your price
range. The overriding consideration for most people, especially beginners, is price, after all, and this will pretty much decide the quality of
frame that you get. But (there is always a but!), when you're shopping

for a frame, you need to look deeper than the paint job and decals, and even the price tag, because you might find that two manufacturers are offering the same basic frame, the same material, dimensions, geometry, and weight, but at two different price points. The main reason for this will be the finish—a fancy paint job and design will add to the price without adding to the ride quality—but the marketing strategy of the company also plays a big role.

Everyone who has shopped for a 'cross frame has heard tales about the claims of some smaller brands that their frame comes out of the same factory as some flashy, more expensive model. The only difference, according to these claims, is the paint. Can that be true, or is it some urban myth? It turns out that in some cases, it is indeed true. That classy Italian model that looks so perfect may be very similar to a more basic-looking frame; it just costs a few hundred or thousand dollars (or euros) more. There are only so many factories producing bike frames, and quite a high percentage of these are in the Far East. So you might find that getting a frame with a slightly plainer finish can save you some money while providing the same level of performance.

So what should you look for in a 'cross frame? Fit is the most important factor. If you already own a road bike and it fits you comfortably, then go for the same sizing. In fact, check to see if your road bike brand makes a 'cross frame, as manufacturers tend to have a sizing philosophy that applies to their entire range of products. If the road bike fits you nicely, then chances are the 'cross frame will too.

If you have only ridden a mountain bike, if this is your first bike, or if you are still growing and not quite sure what size to get, then you need the services of your local bike shop. The advice you get from knowledgeable staff at a local shop can be invaluable, and it will probably be free, so repay them with some loyalty and business; you might find the same equipment on the Internet, and maybe even at a lower price, but on the Internet you won't get the advice and investment of time that a store's staff can offer. In the long run, the bike shop staff might save you money because they'll keep you from spending it on the wrong stuff.

Once you know the size you want, look at the geometry and the 'cross specificity of the frame. Some frames that are marketed as 'cross frames can also be used for winter training on the road or for touring. They will invariably have bottle-cage bosses on the seat and down tubes and most likely eyes for mudguards or fenders, and baggage racks, on the wheel dropouts. There is nothing wrong with this; the extra few bits add negligible weight, and it does mean you can use the same bike out of season and carry a bottle, or stick some road wheels in and use it with a set of fenders for winter training. So give these frames careful consideration. If the bike is going to be 'cross only—no compromise—then these features will not be for you. A sign of a serious frame is that these add-ons will not be present.

Cantilever brakes are always a must; you need the stopping power and the extra mud clearance they provide. So make sure any frame you purchase has cantilever brake bosses. The second must-have is a replaceable rear derailleur hanger. It is highly likely that at some point you will take part in such a muddy race that your derailleur gets clogged and swings over the top of your sprockets, damaging the hanger as it does. While a replaceable one costs very little, and it's just a five-minute job to replace it, a broken, nonreplaceable hanger probably means a new frame.

You also need clearance around the rear wheel, so if possible, ask to see the frame with a pair of wheels in it (complete with tires). Check the space between the tire and the back of the bottom bracket, and also between the side of the tire and the chainstays. With the front wheel in, check the shape of the top of the forks and see if there is adequate clearance. While you have the wheels in, it's not a bad idea just to measure the bottom bracket height to see if it has been built to provide some extra ground clearance. Measure from a level floor to the center of the bottom bracket shell; it should be around 280 millimeters.

This is the reason you need a bike with good clearance!

Frame angles, which affect the handling of the bike, vary from one manufacturer to the next, but most reduce the head tube angle by a degree or so over a road frame of a similar size, so most tend to be 72 to 72.5 degrees. This effectively lengthens the front end of the bike, reduces pedal overlap of the front wheel, and makes cornering at slower speeds more precise. Seat angles also vary. Alan still uses a 74-degree seat, but many other manufacturers use a 73-degree seat, which produces a riding position slightly farther back over the rear wheel. This feature can improve traction.

The next consideration—and the one that has the biggest impact on price—is the material the frame is made from. Nowadays that is likely to be aluminum or carbon, but a few manufacturers are also making 'cross frames from titanium. There are still some small custom builders using steel, but price for weight they are outshone by aluminum every time. Both aluminum and carbon come in a variety of weights, grades, and qualities, and these differences are usually reflected in the price. The cheaper the frame, the thicker the walls of the tubes, and therefore the heavier it will be. And with extra tube thickness and weight also comes a reduction in the quality of the "feel" of the bike; a bike with a heavier frame won't accelerate or be as lively as one built with a better-quality tube set.

One downside of a high-quality light alloy frame is that the tube walls are so thin that it's possible to squeeze the tube with your fingers; when a frame is this soft, it's susceptible to damage when you crash, which you will be doing when you ride 'cross. Even handlebars swinging around and banging the top tube can leave a dent. Carbon, in contrast, is structurally tougher but equally light, as is titanium. Carbon and titanium frames are, however, more expensive. The choice is yours!

So which brands should you look out for? If you want to purchase a bike from one of the major manufacturers, or like the idea of buying a complete off-the-peg bike, then look no further than the names that started the mountain-bike revolution. Trek, Specialized, Cannondale, Scott, and Kona all have great machines, as does Focus, which, in Europe at least, has very well-specced, low- and middle-priced complete bikes.

If you want to build your own bike, starting with a frame, then Ridley is probably the current must-have brand, with models in aluminum and carbon. In fact, five Elite World Championships over the past six years have been won on Ridley frames. But there is an abundance of quality frames out there. Alan frames, the original Italian favorite, are still as good as they ever were, but the jewel is probably the Colnago C50. The frame of choice of the Dutch Rabobank squad and Sven Nys, it's not the lightest or the trickest, but in the words of a very famous European beer commercial, "it's reassuringly expensive!"

It almost seems a shame to get it dirty; the Colnago
C50 is the bike of choice for Sven Nys.

THE FORK

The fork is now considered a separate component, so it's possible to
upgrade a budget frame that came with a cheaper one, or specifically
pick a fork to go with a frame. Carbon is the material of choice, and
even some budget forks come with carbon legs. I would recommend
going with a brand name you can trust when choosing a fork; the consequences of fork breakages tend to be pretty messy, especially if you
value your teeth and nose. Cyclocross is tough on equipment, so it is
wise to replace the fork every couple of seasons to avoid failure from
built-up fatigue. You can, however, save a significant amount of
weight with a nice fork for a reasonable cost, so check out the market.

Most people looking for a fork want to know whether to get the
straight blade or curved type. It actually makes very little difference to
the ride of the bike which type you get. Straight is probably more popular at the moment. But do remember to get the correct diameter
steerer tube to match your frame's head tube.

One name to look for is the Python, made by Ridley under its 4ZA brand, which probably has the lowest height (388 mm) of any fork on the market at the moment. It is also one of the lightest forks on the market (430 g). The Alpha Q (395 mm/455 g), the Easton (485 g), the Reynolds Ouzo Pro (395 mm/490 g), and the Alan (550 g) are all good-quality forks as well.

THE HEADSET

The frame should be finished off with a good-quality headset. Headsets are often overlooked but vital to the ride. The bottom race of a headset is continually bombarded with water and crud off the front wheel, which ruins bearings quickly. Moreover, a headset that is loose or worn will rattle on bumpy descents and adversely affect braking, whereas too tight a headset will affect steering and general balance. The style—that is, whether it is a conventional, integrated, or internal design—will be determined by your frame and fork. You can rely on Cane Creek or the aptly named Chris King to give you the best service, or check out the new FSA Orbit, which has a front canti-cable guide integrated into the top cap—very cool.

Components

WHEELS

The most important component on the bike is undoubtedly the wheel/tire combination. Remember when the choice was pretty simple? You'd pick suitable rims, hubs, and spokes; find a good wheel builder to make the components into a finished article; and go race 'em. Then Mavic started the ball rolling with complete wheel sets, everyone else followed, and now you have wheels to cater to every kind of event and every size of wallet.

Conventionally spoked wheels are still out there, and they're still a good choice for riders who like to replace rims when needed or who enjoy building their own wheels. They're also still relatively affordable. But with wheel packages coming down in price and the number of choices rising steadily upward, budget will be the determining factor. One recommendation can be made with certainty: Look for the lightest wheels you can afford, as wheel/tire weight, more than any other factor, will affect speed on your bike. It's worth the investment to get the best ones you can justify for your budget.

At this point, you must decide whether you are going to race on tubular tires (sew-ups) or clinchers, as this will influence the type of wheels you are going to need. Clinchers are cheaper, more serviceable, and more readily available than sew-ups; they're also easy to repair if you puncture them and are available in more weights and tread patterns—but they are slower. Sew-ups are more expensive, harder to get hold of, messier to work with, harder to repair when punctured, and only available in limited sizes and tread designs—but faster. Hey, no one said it was going to be easy! In the next section, we'll discuss the actual tires. For now we are talking wheels, and in general, clincher wheels are heavier than wheels for sew-ups at an equivalent quality.

One consideration when deciding on wheels is the compatibility of everything you are going to use. If you decide to train on clinchers, then race on sew-ups, make sure the rim sections are the same so you don't have to adjust brakes every time you change wheels. This means you will be able to use the clinchers as spares during races without problems. It also goes without saying that you should make sure you have the same type of cassettes on all your wheels so you don't have to constantly adjust gears; and don't try to mix 10-speed with 9-speed, because it simply won't work.

If you look at photos of the top guys and girls racing, you will see an abundance of deep-section carbon rims being used. In deep mud and sand, the deep rims track better and allow more precise steering than standard low rims. When the ground conditions go over the top of the rim, the action of the spokes cutting through it seriously affects

A fast tire on one of the fastest wheels. The Dugast Rhino has a tread pattern that can cope with muddy conditions and a light supple casing that can be run at low pressures. Stuck onto a deep-section carbon-rimmed wheelset, they make a big difference on your bike and, more importantly, your performance.

steering on the front wheel, and also drags your speed down. Although there are some deep aluminum rims on the market, they are quite heavy. If your choice is heavy and deep or lighter and low, I'd suggest lighter and low, but if you can stretch to deep-section carbon, then go for it. Brands to look for are Reynolds, Easton, Bontrager, Zipp, and Vuelta, as well as the big-name but more expensive Shimano and Campagnolo. Weights tend to be from 1,200 to 1,500 grams for models from the companies above, whereas clinchers come in weights around 1,500 to 1,900 grams. If you decide on clinchers, then Mavic, with plenty of choices offered, is probably the market leader, closely followed by Bontrager, Cane Creek, and FSA.

Be aware that if you intend to compete in UCI races, you will have to follow UCI rules on wheels. The rules state that any wheel with a rim depth of more than 2.5 centimeters or with fewer than sixteen spokes has to have been impact-tested. You can find an up-to-date list of the wheels that have passed this test on the UCI Web site at www.uci.ch.

TIRES

As mentioned above, you will have to decide whether to use clinchers or tubulars, or a combination of the two. One option is to train on clinchers and race on tubulars.

Clinchers are more popular than tubulars because of their wide availability and convenience. It's simple economics. If you get a flat on a clincher, unless you actually split a sidewall or put a hole in the casing, it is going to be easy to repair or replace the inner tube. If you do the same on a tubular, replacing and resticking it are an expensive, time-consuming operation.

That said, in my opinion, the ride offered by a tubular is far superior to that of a clincher, and in 99 percent of situations, big races are still going to be won on a glued-on tire. Fat clinchers offer their biggest advantages on very rocky or icy ground, or during training, when they are simple to repair if you should flat. Otherwise, they simply do not perform as well as tubulars. The supple casing of a tub allows more of the tread to stay in contact with the ground, resulting in better traction, and with more tread able to follow any irregularities on the terrain, steering and control are kept at a premium. To have a similar effect with a clincher, the tire pressure has to be too low and pinch flats occur, a common problem with a clincher but much rarer on a tubular unless you really hit a rock, root, or curb with some force.

Now that a good variety of clinchers are available, the number of choices can be bewildering. The two main factors are tread pattern and size. As a general rule, if you are using the same wheels and tires for all conditions, go for something in the 28- to 32-millimeter range. Avoid anything narrower than 28 mm, and only use a tire wider than 34 mm if you are sure you have the clearance available on your frame. But as those nice guys at the UCI have also ordained, 35 mm is the maximum size allowed in UCI races, and that kind of limits you. It's also worth noting that when race officials check tire width, as they did at the most recent World Championships as riders went to staging, they use a 35 mm gauge, and if it doesn't slip over the tire, then you need a quick wheel change or you don't start. The size that the tire manufacturer prints on the sidewall is irrelevant, so unfortunately you can't use that as justification for a wider tire. Most clinchers come in this size range, and the best of these come from Michelin, especially the Mud2, the Maxxis, the Hutchinson, the Schwalbe, and the Ritchey. Don't forget to use an inner tube that is compatible in size with the clincher tire you are using. Do not be tempted to use standard road tubes, as these are too narrow and will have to stretch too much to fill the space. Instead, fit a 28 to 35 mm tube. Also, make sure you fit a high-quality rim strip, either the one recommended by your wheel manufacturer, which will usually come with the wheels, or any brand that gives a tight fit, that will not expand or move when wet, and that covers the spoke holes completely.

If you decide to race on tubulars, then the choice comes down to about half a dozen brands and, in reality, only two distinct tread patterns. You have two options: the long-appreciated chevron tread, which can be used for the majority of conditions, or a mud option when conditions get too slippery for the chevrons. You might occasionally find a file tread, but these tubulars are so specialized that it's generally not worth the hassle of gluing them on, and they're only useful on icy or extremely smooth surfaces or sand.

As for width, don't go below 30 mm, and try to go with 32 mm. This is the current favorite and can be used in most conditions. The wider size, 34 mm, is for those days when it's very sandy; when it's frozen, rutted, and bumpy; or when you get a chance to race in the Netherlands on their sandy courses. The 34 mm tires provide extra cushion to reduce the bouncing around, and they allow you to race with very low tire pressure to maximize grip.

Look for selections from Challenge (formerly Clément), which makes the long-famous Grifo with the original chevron tread in 30, 32, and 34 mm, now with an additional row of small knobs around the sidewall to give really great cornering traction. Tufo, the brand from the Czech Republic, is the only tubular out there without an inner tube; Vittoria, another classy Italian name from the past, has recently updated its Cross Evo range; and the daddy of them all, the Dugast range, comes from Holland.

The Tufo is the most interesting of these choices. As Tufos do not have a tube, you can run them at low pressure without fear of pinch-flatting, and if you do cut the carcass or tread and puncture them, you can reseal them with any of the liquid latex sealants on the market, most of which are sold to seal tubeless mountain-bike tires. The last name on that list, Dugast, is well-known to longtime 'cross riders. As romantic as the image might be of an aging Frenchman lovingly hand-crafting 'cross tubulars in his back room, the reality is that the name and machinery were relocated to the Netherlands a few years ago, and now Dutchman Richard Nieuwhuis is the man in charge of a company that operates on a much more commercial basis than back in the day of old Monsieur Dugast. The Dugast range is the only one at the moment with the standard chevron design (the Typhoon) as well as a specific mud tread (the Rhino), and both are available in 32 mm and 34 mm widths. Used by a large percentage of the pro 'cross world in Europe, Dugast tires are the lightest and fastest ones out there and are now also more affordable than in the past; however, the quality has come down slightly to reflect the price and mass production.

There are two things that are just as important as the type of tires you use: how you stick them on, and the pressures at which you run them while racing. The majority of 'cross racers inflate their tires too hard because they fail to consider the course surface. But using tires at lower pressures requires that they be properly glued on, especially nowadays when tires up to 35 mm wide can be used on regular road

HOW TO GLUE A TUBULAR ONTO A CARBON RIM

If you start with a new carbon rim, you must first roughen up the surface to be glued with a rough sand paper or emery paper, and then degrease the rim so there is no dust or anything left over from the rim mold that will affect the glue. Then start with the glue: Spread one thin layer onto the rim and put the wheel to one side for a minimum of one day. Repeat that process with another thin layer, and again leave the wheel for at least one day.

Next, check the fit of the tubular onto the rim; if the center of the rim is so deep that the entire base tape of the tubular does not touch the rim, you need to fill in the gap in the center. To do that, use a half-width base tape from an old tubular: Add a layer of glue and then stick on the half-width tape, and then add another layer of glue on top of that, and again leave it for a day.

The next thing is to put a layer of glue on the base tape of the tubular (inflate the tire slightly so it turns inside out), apply a final layer of glue on the rim, and within ten minutes mount the tubular on the rim.

My number one choice for glue is Continental, number two is Vittoria. At Dugast we are developing a new glue in conjunction with 3M which, when it is ready, will mean a much faster assembly of the tubular onto the rim, possibly within six hours.

You can't put layers of glue onto the tire the same way as the rim because it makes the base tape very hard and inelastic, and as you must stretch the tubular onto the rim you risk breaking the base tape, which ruins the tire.

So there you have it. The golden rule is lots of thin layers with a lot of time between each layer, all on a rim that is rough and absolutely clean, dry, and dust-free. I also stretch the tubular prior to putting glue on the base tape, either by inflating it on an old or spare wheel or rim, or by gently pulling while the other end is hooked under my foot. Do this gently, and do it all around the tubular so it stays round.

RICHARD NIEUWHUIS, DUGAST

rims that are 20 to 22 mm wide and possibly made of shiny, smooth carbon. Otherwise, you are liable to lose them—always at the point farthest from the pit area!

There are two ways to stick a tire to a rim: good old-fashioned glue, or one of the types of tapes that are available. Tape is pretty good on the road or track, but take care using it for 'cross, as it is susceptible to drying out after regular wheel washing or wet races. It is true that glue takes time to apply and is messy, whereas with tape you can have a tire on in two minutes, but glue is worth the hassle in the long run. There are very few mechanical problems during a race that make riding to a pit (and a spare bike) an impossible task, but a broken chain and a rolled tire are two that will stop you dead. So spare no effort in your gluing, and be prepared, as it takes time over a few days to do it correctly.

When you are confident that your tires are glued on securely, you can start racing with them at the correct pressure without fear of rolling them. Your weight and riding style will affect the pressure, as will the ground conditions on the circuit, but experience will tell you what you can get away with. As you get better you will be able to ride softer, as relative 'cross newcomer Thijs Al (who placed third in the World Cup Hofstade and tenth in the World Elite Champs in 2007) has discovered. He said, "I still cannot ride with the same pressures as Groenendaal and De Knegt; if they use 1.4 bars I have to use 1.45 or even 1.5. They can continue to pedal in the corners and the softer tires help a lot, but I'm still learning how to do this and for me, to ride that soft, I'm not good enough yet." A softer tire will improve traction considerably, but 1.4 to 1.5 bars (20–22 psi) is as soft as you will go. And certainly no more than 3 bars (42 psi) will ever be required. Get a track (stand) pump with a reliable gauge or a digital pressure gauge and stick by it. Remember that a 32 mm Dugast with 2 bars (28 psi) in it will feel softer to the squeeze than a Tufo at the same pressure because of their different casings, but do not be tempted to run the Tufo softer.

Tires should be checked meticulously every time the bike is cleaned, both for cuts and to ensure they are still stuck on. If you find a cut in the tread that has not gone through to the carcass, then Super Glue is the best stuff to fill it with. If you find that a tire needs resticking, take it off the rim and dry both overnight before reapplying a layer of glue to both rim and tire and replacing the tire.

Finally, have you noticed how the pros' tubulars always seem clean while your sidewalls are perpetually mud-stained? The Belgians are known to paint their sidewalls with clear neoprene liquid glue, which keeps mud out of the casing and washes clean; the stuff they use is called Bison, but clear Copydex also works.

TRANSMISSION

Gearing is pretty straightforward in these modern times. The basic, most obvious fact is simply that you will need a lower range of gearing than on your road bike. Chainring sizes should be a 39 inner with an outer of either 46 or 48, depending on how fast you like to think you are. Previously the outer was always a 48, but this has come down as sprocket sizes have decreased. A 48/13 of old is actually a slightly lower gear than 46/12, and as the latter is readily available (and also slightly lighter), there is little reason to go back to 48 outer rings. If you struggle to find replacement 46 rings for your current crankset, then check out the range from TA, which offers all sizes for the majority of crank configurations.

The other option is to use a compact crankset, which comes ready to go with smaller rings, usually something like 34/48 or 36/50. Although you probably won't find this combination on the bike of an experienced racer, mainly because the difference between the small ring and the large ring is too great and the setup requires too much gear changing, it will be fine for you if you are starting out. At some point, you will start to wish you had a ring somewhere in between the two; then you will know it's time to go for a more traditional 'cross setup.

The cassette on the back should be from a regular range, and it should be from one of the three main manufacturers: Shimano, Campagnolo, or SRAM. Shimano cassettes tend to have 25 or 27 sprockets, whereas Campagnolo and SRAM cassettes have 26 and 28, but in all likelihood you will have whichever type is compatible with your wheelset or with your shifters and derailleurs. You might encounter a stumbling block if you are trying to use different wheels that you've collected over several years and have to mix and match 9- and 10-speed components. There is slightly more space between sprockets in a 9-speed, so mud may not be as much of an issue as with the 10-speed, but unfortunately, both types are so narrow now that even a relatively clean bike will have to be changed in the pit so the sprockets can be cleaned; otherwise, jumping gears will handicap you.

In the old days, it was common to see 'crossers using a single 42-tooth chainring with chainguards on either side and a 6-speed cluster ranging from 13 to 26; today, with nine or ten cogs at the rear, it makes more sense to run a single ring, as you've got a better range of gears, especially with 11 or 12 top sprockets coming as standard.

A single ring with chainguards offers a lighter, neater alternative to the regular double chainring setup and does away with the need for a front derailleur.

Originally, the main reason for using a single ring and guards was to keep the chain on the ring. In days of old, when derailleurs didn't have such high-quality springs and 26 mm tires didn't soak up much shock from rough ground, chains regularly bounced off. Using a single ring and guards also saved the weight of front gear shifters when they were at the ends of the handlebars, along with a front derailleur and associated cable. Nowadays weight saving is still a worthwhile consideration. Look for carbon guards from FSA, 4ZA, Spooky, or TA, which all manufacture guards for 42 or 44 chainrings in Shimano or Campagnolo pitch. Not only will you save some weight, you'll have a cleaner, neater-looking area around the bracket that will not attract as much mud, and therefore weight.

Whatever system you decide on, make sure you avoid sprockets larger than 28, for two reasons. The main reason is mechanical; no standard rear derailleur will easily accommodate a 30 or 32 sprocket, which require a long-armed mechanism that is susceptible to damage from stray sticks and rocks. Second, if you are traveling slow enough to need 39×32 during a race, you might be better off running.

All modern derailleurs designed for road racing are suitable for 'cross, and all can accept the range of gears mentioned above. Cheaper derailleurs work just as well as the more expensive models when they are new—they are simply heavier and wear out faster. Paying more won't necessarily get you better shifting, but it may get you more of it. A high-quality derailleur will also make the overall package lighter.

While we're on the subject of gears, don't overlook the cables, as these can affect shifting enormously. Gore-Tex cables are very smooth and stay that way for a significantly longer period of time than regular cables; though expensive, they are a worthwhile investment. Make sure the outer cable is in good shape, with well-fitting ferrules, and that there are no splits or kinks that will affect the inner cable run.

Shift levers are now universally integrated into the brake levers. There are three brands to consider: Shimano, Campagnolo, and

SRAM. I have always been a bigger fan of the Italian brand over its Japanese equivalent, as I prefer the neater cable run under the bar tape; in addition, because the whole lever moves on the Shimano, crashes or dropped bikes during changes in the pits invariably mean getting a shifter full of mud or sand, which isn't really a great scenario during a race. A new system from SRAM, in use for the first time during the 2006–2007 'cross season, is worth investigating. It will be interesting to see how it is accepted and how well it copes with the rigors of winter racing. First reports indicate that it is excellent, and in any case the addition of a third type means greater choice for all.

PEDALS

You will notice in the chapters on training and technique just how much emphasis is put on the ability to get your feet back into the pedals after remounting your bike (see Chapter 3). It's a vital technique to nail down, and your choice of pedals and shoes will go at least some of the way toward making it an easier skill to master.

This issue becomes especially important when mud or debris clogs the pedal mechanism or the area around the cleat on the shoe, delaying reentry while you attempt to kick off or stamp out the offending blockage. A pedal system that offers good mud clearance can help to minimize the problem. Shimano started the ball rolling and is still at the forefront of quality in off-road pedal design. The Shimano XTR M-970 model, for example, is top-of-the-line. The mud clearance on a Shimano pedal may not be the best out there, but it's better than it used to be. It's not the lightest pedal either, but the bearings stand up to pressure washers and the spring tension is adjustable. The Time Atac models are also good and have a reputation for great mud clearance. But the new king of 'cross pedals is Crank Brothers, whose Eggbeater and Candy models laugh in the face of mud and sand. The company's flagship models in titanium are also significantly lighter than their competition. The only downside is that they tend to wear

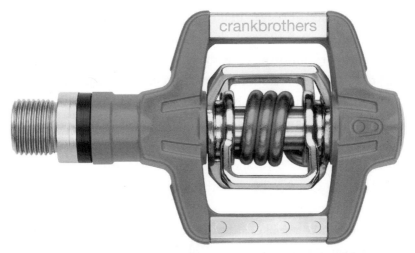

These pedals give great mud clearance. The model with the platform around the mechanism makes it easier for your foot to locate the pedal after a remount.

out the soles of shoes pretty quickly compared with the Shimano and especially the Time models, which have a slightly bigger platform.

Cleats for 'cross now use the same universal two-bolt fastening system used in all off-road shoes. Make sure you change cleats regularly, particularly when they show signs of wear or become harder to disengage from the pedal. Being stuck in your pedals isn't ideal when faced with a set of hurdles at 30 kilometers per hour.

BRAKES

If you are serious about 'cross, you will certainly have a frame with brazed-on pivots for cantilever brakes. No other type of braking system will do. The main advantage of this style of brake is that it does not clog up with mud. It is also a powerful means of slowing down— something you will be very glad of on a descent. Cantilever brakes are light and simple as well. The advent of mountain bikes brought a large number of brake styles and makes onto the market. Some are suitable but others are not, as they are designed to work with a specific lever that is only available for use on straight handlebars.

The original cantilever brakes were the classic Mafac and the Swiss Weinmann 420, and these remained the best cantilever brakes for years; unfortunately, these models have become obsolete and production has ceased. But something based on the same simple design is what you should look for. The closest at the moment to these old faithfuls are models from Frogglegs and Spooky, two European companies. Spooky also has a carbon model for the fashion-conscious consumer. Also look out for Avid Shorty 6 from SRAM and the Cane Creek SCX-6, both of which offer good, basic, no-nonsense brakesets.

Mountain-bike V brakes are rarely suitable, as they are designed for use with a cammed lever, only available in a straight-bar design. Most drop-bar brake levers do not provide enough leverage to work with such cantilevers, and you have to adjust the brake pads very close to the rim; otherwise you may find yourself pulling the lever all the way back to the bars without slowing down.

Most 'cross brakes are supplied with brake pads that work fine on aluminum rims, but when faced with carbon they tend to shy away from their intended purpose, as if it were an intimidating material for a lowly brake pad. Although most carbon wheelsets now come with a set of suitable pads, these are always made to fit cartridge-style road brake shoes, not post-mounted brake shoes. Thankfully, a few manufacturers have realized that this incompatibility exists and are now making pads that will slow down wet, muddy carbon rims. SwissStop, Ritchey, and BBB pads are good examples.

One interesting recent development is the use of an additional set of brake levers on the tops of the bars. This lets a rider brake from a riding position, as if he or she were riding a mountain bike. To try this, simply fit a pair of mountain-bike levers to the tops, close to the stem, with a single cable run through both sets of levers. It adds weight, but if you ride a lot with your hands on the tops, then this technique could be for you. Personally, I don't particularly like top-

Top-mounted brake levers can be a useful addition
if you like to ride on the tops of the bars or if you are
a more cautious descender, as you can stay in a
more upright position, similar to a mountain biker.
Hanka Kupfernagel's bike uses a through cable from
her STI levers.

mounted brake levers; they tend to encourage a riding position that is
uniquely on the tops. After all, if you can brake from there, you only
need to move your hands to change gears—and this position isn't one
that you can use for fast acceleration or correct cornering. And why
cart around that extra weight?

As with gear cables, think about an upgrade on the brake-cable system you use. Gore-Tex makes brake cables with the same advantages as
its gear cables—long, smooth life and a lighter action—and there are
numerous Teflon-coated cablesets around that are worth investigating.

HANDLEBARS, STEMS, SADDLES, AND SEAT POSTS

Bars come in a variety of widths and styles. The best shape for 'cross is anything with a relatively square, shallow design with enough of a flat top section to grab on to using a wide hand position, which promotes good control. The shallow drop does not mean a vastly different position for the short periods of time that you're riding on the bottom part of the bars.

Carbon bars won't bend when you crash or drop bikes while changing, but as with anything carbon, cracks appear when the material is stressed, and breakages, when they do occur, tend to be sudden and drastic. So if you do go with carbon bars, keep an eye on them (and an ear out for any new sounds), and replace them regularly.

Buy stems that match your bars to get an exact fit; other factors include length, rise (or drop) so you can fine-tune your riding position, and weight. Weight is usually reflected in the price.

Saddle technology has gone through the roof in the past few years. New designs, new materials to bring the weight down, and every conceivable design and color are available (to match your frame color or team kit—or even hair color and makeup). Weight and comfort are the critical factors here, along with a covering that is going to be easy to take care of and will not hold water. Rails of aluminum and titanium are great for saving weight. But with the constant jumping onto the bike that cyclocross requires, some of the cheaper models just bend too easily, and a bent saddle can cause major biomechanical problems if you continue to ride on it. Titanium is strong and light, and market leaders such as Selle San Marco and Selle Italia make a huge range of saddles in all sorts of shapes and sizes to suit. You will not be sitting down for hours on end like a road rider, so you can sacrifice a bit of comfort if it will save you some weight.

One quick word on seat posts: Unlike road cycling, which puts very little stress on a seat post, 'cross includes frequent mounting and dismounting. This constant jumping onto the seat means that you must make sure you get a reliable model that will not break. The clamp should remain tight and never slip. And if you use carbon, make sure you have an offset seat clamp on your frame to avoid cracking the post. I'll leave you to imagine the consequences of a seat post breaking when you jump on. . . .

Position on a 'Cross Bike

If you've been cycling on the road for a while before beginning cyclocross, you most likely already have your position sorted out on your road bike. Let's look at how 'cross will affect this position and what changes you'll need to consider that affect how you set up your bike.

Seemingly minor alterations in position can be important because they provide better control and traction. Ideally, you should use a position about 1 centimeter shorter in reach than on your road bike, and either the same, or no more than 1 cm lower, in saddle height. The best way to achieve this is to use a frame smaller by these measurements. You'll be able to use the same-length stem and have the same amount of seat post showing as on your road bike, but the slightly smaller frame will be better for bike handling.

Position your brake levers and bars slightly higher, and set your saddle slightly farther back to give yourself a more upright position over the rear wheel. This change will improve traction in slippery conditions. You might also want to use slightly longer cranks than on your road bike. As in mountain biking, you will be effectively pedaling more slowly in a relatively big gear, and the extra leverage provided by longer cranks can be a real help. Mountain bikes invariably come with 175 mm cranks as standard. If you regularly ride a mountain bike with 175 mm cranks but a road bike with 172.5 mm cranks, then go for 175 mm on your 'cross bike. If you are small, or if you use

U23 World Champion in 2007 Lars Boom shows great body position with hands on the brake levers. With his elbows bent and an aero position he is able to concentrate on maximum speed on this section of the course, and by simply straightening his arms and becoming more upright he is ready to deal with the next corner.

170 mm on the road, use 172.5 mm on your 'cross bike. Anything longer than 175 mm will create problems with ground clearance.

Saving Weight

Saving weight has become the Holy Grail of off-road riders. Mountain bikes now weigh less than road bikes did just a few years ago, and the advantages of low weight, especially for a 'cross bike that you have to pick up and carry uphill, are obvious.

Saving weight on a bike is a bit like buying a better sound system. With the sound system you have to pay twice as much to get a slight improvement in the sound quality. Likewise, you can cut a bike's weight to 17 pounds with relative ease, but to knock another pound off you will have to spend a lot of time and money.

There's no doubt about it: Because of mountain-bike technology and new developments in the road-bike market, you can find a lighter alternative for every component on your 'cross bike, from rims and tires to chainring bolts and handlebar tape, but all at a price. If money is no object, then replace your regular bolts with titanium, buy Ti-rail saddles, get the lightest tires, and help the carbon trade with wheels, cranks, bars, and stems. Just remember that although titanium and carbon are lighter and stronger than virtually every other material, you still need a reliable bike that isn't going to let you down during a race. So check out each part you buy and make sure you know it is going to be reliable.

Care of Equipment

Any good-quality racing bike is an expensive piece of equipment; if looked after correctly, it will not let you down during a race and should last for a few seasons. If taking good care of the equipment is essential for road bikes, it's even more essential for cyclocross bikes.

Out in all weather, continually battered by the terrain, and in need of frequent washes, the life of a 'cross bike, compared with its road-racing cousin, will be a short one. So it is even more important to make sure the level of care is 100 percent at all times.

Try to keep one bike purely for racing and one for training, for pre-race warm-ups, and as a spare during races. It is this training bike that is going to get the most use, but because it is being used frequently, it is easy to take for granted. Try to put aside some time each week to prepare your equipment. Probably the best day is Friday, which is a light training day. That way, you'll have Saturday to get to the bike shop, should you need to. Do not wait until Saturday night to discover that you have a broken seat post when you are supposed to be leaving for a race at 9 A.M. the next day.

Your preparation for the next race starts as soon as the last one is over. While you are getting changed, your helper should clean both bikes as well as possible and load up the car. When you get home, give the bikes a quick squirt of oil on the chains and put them to bed—and do the same yourself! Do not feel obliged to spend another hour in the yard with a bucket; you will be tired after a hard race, so look after yourself first and save the bikes until Monday, when they should be cleaned thoroughly, dried, oiled, and given a quick once-over (for more on cleaning the bike, see the next section). Friday's check will include a more intensive look at the components.

Although you should maintain your bikes throughout the racing season, it's worth putting aside a weekend to give both of them a thorough overhaul. This could be a weekend when you've scheduled a rest from training. Replace the chains, brake pads, and all inner and outer cables; regrease the headsets, bottom brackets, and freehub bodies; reglue the tires; and clean all the components and grease all the threads. This is also a good time for a cleat replacement. Finally, roll on some new clean handlebar tape. If you do this full service a few weeks before a major season goal, you will know that your bike is in the best possible condition for the race. Everything has been fitted and tried and tested prior to your big day, you'll have time to break in your new cleats, and you can be sure your bike won't let you down.

CLEANING A 'CROSS BIKE

Because of the conditions that cyclocross bikes are subjected to, it is important that they be kept clean. This will prolong the life of the components and make any maintenance a lot easier and more pleasant to carry out.

You should try to get into the habit of washing your bike after every training ride and as soon as possible after a race. If you get into a routine, it will not take long. If the bike is especially muddy, use a pressure washer or hose to get rid of most of the mud, then put it on a bike stand to clean it properly. With all the water your bike will be subjected to, especially if you use a pressure washer, you must keep an eye on the main bearings and regrease them regularly; otherwise they will not last long and will have to be replaced too often. Try to avoid directing the blast from a pressure washer straight at a bearing, such as the bottom bracket or sides of the hubs. Try to clean these parts from above, where the water cannot be forced into the moving parts quite so easily. Start cleaning with a pressure washer from the top of the bike and work down, then get your buckets for the next stage.

You will need two buckets of water, preferably hot, one soapy, one not; a stiff dustpan brush; a sponge; and degreaser in either a sprayer or a container with a brush. Any mild dish detergent should be suitable for the soapy water. There are plenty of citrus-based, water-soluble degreasers available, and they are clean and easy to use. Again, try not to spray degreaser directly into hubs or the bottom bracket when you are cleaning the chainrings and sprockets; direct the squirt from above.

With the bike on a stand, degrease the chain, sprockets, and chainrings, and then drop the wheels out. Keep the chain under tension with a "sleeping hub" that fits into the dropout. Scrub the wheels and tires with the stiff brush to remove all the mud, then rinse off the wheels and sprockets with clean water. Then, starting at the top of the bike and working downward, use the hot water and sponge. If the mud has dried, you will probably need the stiff brush, especially around the brakes and pedals, to loosen the mud before cleaning them properly with the sponge. Do not forget to clean under the saddle with the brush; you will be amazed at how much mud ends up under there.

By the time you get to the transmission, the degreaser will have worked its magic and loosened up the oil, most of which will have been washed off by the water you've splashed onto the frame. Fill the sponge with water and run the chain through it while turning the pedals, then rinse the chainrings and derailleurs. Finally, wash the soap off with clean water. Now the bike is ready to be dried and checked over.

CHECKING THE BIKE

Checking your bike for problems will not take long, but be methodical; if you take it step by step, you're less likely to miss anything.

For your weekly check, look for anything that is worn, loose and rattling, or stiff, and service or replace it immediately. The transmission is in for a hard time, so chains should be changed regularly—certainly no less than three times a season, and more if you have a heavy race schedule, encounter a run of bad weather, or happen to live in a particularly sandy area. There is a false economy in continuing to ride with a worn chain, as it will wear out the chainrings and sprockets more rapidly. This can turn into an expensive trip to the bike shop. In addition, gear jockey wheels do not last long under wet, gritty conditions, and if they are worn they can make gear changes difficult. You will certainly need to replace brake pads and all cables from time to time.

This is it for the weekly check, but don't forget the major overhaul mentioned above (under "Care of Equipment"), which should be done a couple of weeks before a major race of the season.

Clothing

The clothing requirements for a 'cross racer do not differ greatly from those of a road racer, but as all your training and racing take place during the coldest, wettest months of the year, you will need some warmer pieces. Good-quality cycling clothes can make all the difference between a productive training session and a miserable, wet ride where the object is simply to get home. For racing, the clothing must be well-fitting, comfortable, and suitable for any extremes of climate.

FOOTWEAR

Starting at the bottom and working up, undoubtedly the most important item of clothing is the footwear. We have the mountain bike to thank for the current wide range of shoes designed for off-road riding. The requirements for a good cyclocross shoe are not necessarily the same as those for a good mountain-bike shoe, however, so check out all the options before deciding. As with all shoes, good fit is crucial.

Some mountain-bike shoes are too stiff for 'cross because in 'cross you must cover sections of the terrain that are slippery on foot. Try to find a shoe with the following features: a slightly more flexible sole at the front to help with any sections you need to cover on foot, screw-in studs or spikes at the very front of the sole, and a fastening system that will not be affected by mud. A lot of very good shoes seem to have been designed in areas where it doesn't rain—90 percent of the shoe is perfect, but it fastens with a Velcro strap that works fine in the dry but comes undone as soon as it becomes wet. The sole should accept the cleat for the style of pedal you have chosen with enough space around it to reduce clogging. It should have an aggressive tread for slippery conditions, but ideally in a grippy, softer material, and it should have removable studs or spikes in the toe for running up hills. If two bikes are a good idea, two pairs of shoes are an even better one. Use one pair to train and warm up in, and then a nice, clean, dry pair

to race in. In this way, last year's racing shoes become this year's training shoes, and so on. Socks should be cotton or a cotton mix rather
than anything shiny or super-stretchy like Lycra or nylon. The
stretchy fabrics are too slippery in your shoes and don't allow your feet
to breathe. Also avoid cushion-soled sport socks, which can hold too
much water. Your socks should be short and well-fitting. Don't forget
to wear racing socks when you try on shoes—a good-fitting shoe is essential. A shoe that is too big can get stuck in the mud and come off;
one that is too tight may constrict your toes and/or stop the blood
flow to your toes when it gets cold.

SHORTS AND SKINSUITS

Shorts should either be part of a skinsuit or of the bib variety. Lycra is
the norm, but as this comes in a variety of qualities that affect the fit,
choose carefully. Also look for a synthetic chamois insert that can be
machine washed and will dry quickly.

Shorts are your most important point of contact with the bike;
they must fit perfectly and always be clean. Even a slight problem can
manifest itself as a saddle sore, which invariably means time off the
bike to allow for healing. So do not skimp on this purchase.

Skinsuits are the most popular form of race clothing, in either long
or short sleeves, depending on the temperature. They provide a good
fit and don't become baggy when wet. During the early season, you
can probably get away with wearing a summer undervest under your
skinsuit. This should be one of the base-layer garments that wick per-
spiration from your skin to the outer surface, where it can evaporate
quickly, leaving you warm and dry. To do this, the undervest must be
close-fitting and have some stretch to it.

As winter sets in you will need either more under the skinsuit or a
skinsuit made of a warmer material. Thermo-Lycra with a slight fleecy
back is readily available from quality clothing manufacturers. Interest-
ingly, some skinsuits that the Rabobank guys use when it turns cold

It's important to be well dressed on the start line so you begin the race as warm as possible. The same goes for the riders!

have a toweling insert in place of the more normal chamois style, which does not hold water when it's wet and muddy. If you stick with standard Lycra, then keep the undervest as the base layer and add a mid-layer to trap body heat and keep you insulated from the cold. This mid-layer can be either another standard base layer—maybe a long-sleeved version of the summer one—or a winter base layer that is slightly thicker and warmer. Remember, most of these types of garments are not windproof (although some are available with a windproof covering on the front), so if the wind is biting, make sure you have something on that will give you some protection, even if it is just a sheet of plastic or bubble wrap under your skinsuit.

If the temperature drops below freezing, or if you are racing in the snow, always wear knee warmers or leg warmers on top of embrocation. And definitely wear some chest protection under your skinsuit—either a vest made for the purpose or a do-it-yourself version made out of bubble wrap.

GLOVES

Something should always be worn on the hands, no matter what the weather. Short-fingered mitts or full-fingered gloves are both options. You will be falling off at some point during the season, and as hands are usually one of the body parts that hit the ground in a fall, you need some measure of protection. Gloves or mitts also provide better grip on wet bar tape, help with picking up the bike, and are even useful for wiping mud off your face so you look good when you cross the finish line. There are plenty of thermal gloves on the market, but many are too slippery on the handlebars or become ineffective when they get wet. Ski gloves are very warm and usually have some degree of water resistance, but they tend to be bulky, which can be awkward for braking and gear shifting. Gloves made out of Gore-Tex or similar materials are by far the best, although thin neoprene material is also very effective in cold, wet conditions.

Some gloves and mitts have a nonslip grip on the palm and/or a long wrist section to fill the gap that can occur between glove and jersey. These are both useful features. Wear your watch or heart rate monitor over the top of your jersey sleeve so that you can see at a glance how long you have been riding without having to push your sleeve up.

HEADGEAR AND EYEWEAR

Helmets are obligatory in races worldwide, and since you have to wear one, it may as well be a good one. Helmets seem to be more "hole" than "helmet" nowadays as manufacturers strive to minimize helmet weight and maximize summertime cooling properties. This is great for people who ride primarily in the summertime, but you will need to find something to wear under your helmet to keep your head warm; a tremendous amount of heat is lost through the head on cold days. Wearing a purpose-made skullcap or roadie-style cap underneath will keep some of the heat in. Also on wet days, have the peak of a cap down at the front to help keep water out of your eyes.

Use eyewear if the conditions are exceptionally cold or wet or are an extreme of light, be it dull or bright. Eyewear is also useful if you are racing in sand, as it can save you from getting your eyes full of the stuff off the wheel in front of you. Along with protecting your eyes from cold and wet conditions and grit—and that rare winter commodity, sunshine—specific lenses can brighten up the dull or flat light common to a wooded area, especially when you're in the last race of the day as dusk falls. If the ground is wet and muddy, chances are your glasses are not going to stay clean much past the first lap. But even if you simply wear them for the initial starting effort, when water splashing out from under the wheels of others in the group can be an inconvenience, and then throw them off to your pit crew, it will be worth the effort.

In mountain-bike races, eyewear changes are regularly done in the feed or "pit" areas; however, successfully changing a bike and glasses each lap is not practical. Wear the glasses as long as they are effective, and then get rid of them.

WARM-UP GEAR

Warming up before a race means just that—getting your body warm—so dress accordingly. In general, it's better to wear too much than not enough.

For your pre-race course examination, don your spare shoes and overshoes, your warm training tights and tops, a rain jacket, if required, plus your helmet and spare gloves. If it's a very wet circuit or it's raining when you pre-ride, also wear waterproof over-trousers, ideally with a tapered leg or taped so they don't catch in your chainrings.

Before the start, once you have changed into your race clothes, put your extra jacket back on, and also your tights or leg warmers, if you can get them off easily without removing your shoes. These can be discarded at the last minute right at the starting line to avoid too much cooling off.

One very useful addition to your bag is a pair of "tear-off" tights or leg warmers with full-length zips, which can be left on until the last minute before the start, then removed easily and quickly. Bio Racer makes the ones that the Belgians use, but other clothing manufacturers are gradually adding them to their product lines.

TRAINING GEAR

Your training gear will be very similar to the clothing you train in all year. But remember, you will be out in all types of weather, and bad weather—fog and ice excepted—is no reason to miss a training session.

In extremes of cold and wet, wearing a number of thin layers will keep you warmer than just one or two thick items—and as long as you are warm, getting wet is not a problem. Pay special attention to the extremities—head, hands, and feet. Good overshoes, gloves, and a hat will reduce heat loss dramatically. And good-quality base layers, as mentioned earlier, plus long johns in the same material, good-quality tights and jackets, thermal suits, and rain jackets in modern fabrics should see you through all but the harshest winter weather.

If you train in the evenings, make sure you are visible to traffic by wearing light-colored clothing for the last layer or some sort of reflective outerwear. Also be sure that your training bike has a good lighting system and reflectors, plus fenders to keep water off your back and legs.

Eyewear is always a good idea for training. Use clear, red, or yellow lenses, which will brighten up dull light conditions and keep water, snow, and grit out of your eyes. Glasses also help keep your face warm if the wind is particularly biting.

Fleece neck warmers are a great winter accessory as well and make a huge difference in your comfort level on the bike. They keep the cold air from going down the collar of your jacket and can be pulled up to your nose to keep your chin and cheeks warm.

RUNNING GEAR

The last set of training gear you will need to think about is for running. As you will see in Chapter 4, running should play a significant part in your schedule, so do not treat it as an afterthought.

You will not have to wear as much clothing for running as you do on the bike. Your body generates more heat while running, and there is a lower windchill factor in running because you are not traveling as fast. However, you will also sweat a lot more, so the first layer should always be one of the base-layer undervests we have already discussed to wick away moisture. On top of this, cycling tops or jackets are fine as long as they are roomier and not too restrictive.

Breathable running suits made out of Gore-Tex or something similar are ideal if you run a lot. They are totally weatherproof, but unlike a standard rain suit, they do not leave you feeling as though you have been training in the sauna. These suits will make the majority of winter runs a whole lot more enjoyable, leaving you with no excuse for any missed training sessions. But they will not double as cycling garments, since they are designed and cut for running.

Finally, be sure to get the right running shoes, even though it will take some time to find the ones that are best for you—and even though they will be more expensive than shoes from your local big-box superstore. You may not consider yourself a runner, but a good pair of shoes is the most crucial item for your training runs. Find a shop that specializes in running shoes that has a staff made up of runners, even if it is just for your first pair, to get the correct model and size. Explain how far you are running and on what types of surfaces, and spend time trying on different makes and models.

If the majority of your running will be on grass, go for a suitable cross-country-style shoe. This will give you the required grip and support to cope with the stress of off-road running. This type of shoe will not be suitable for running on roads, as the sole will be too slippery and there will not be enough cushioning. If you run on the road, go for a road training shoe. This is where you need the specialists' advice—the running-shoe market is massive, catering to a vast range of fitness levels, abilities, physiques, and types of racing or training. Narrowing down the choices may even be worse than buying your first bike!

Embrocation

Almost as important as the clothing you wear to race in, and certainly as important in your battle to keep warm, is the embrocation you use. Embrocation is a cream, oil, or petroleum jelly–based product that many racers use on their legs to gain some protection from the elements. In some cases, depending on the ingredients in the product, embrocation can stimulate an increase in blood flow to promote the efficiency of the muscles and keep them warm. When a muscle is warm, it works better and the risk of pulls, tears, cramps, and strains is reduced.

Much depends on the weather. As a general rule, creams such as Born, Musclor, and Radian, or light oils such as Sixtus, should be used if it is cold but dry. But these will not be as effective in wet conditions. If it is wet, either cover them with an oil or use a petroleum-based embrocation such as Cramer or Sports Balm, which will not wash off. The bigger names in embrocation usually offer a range of products suitable for all the conditions you are likely to race in. For example, the Dutch brand Born has creams with different warming properties depending on the air temperature, protective oils that go on top of the cream to protect you from rain and cold, plus sports washes that get it all off and after-race massage oils that aid muscle recovery.

Do not limit their use to your legs; if it is very wet and cold, use a warm cream on your lower back, arms, feet, and hands. The warmer you start the race, the more of a chance you have of staying comfortable throughout. And cold feet and hands can be miserable, diverting attention from the job at hand.

Remember that embrocations designed to stay on' in wet weather will not wash off easily in the shower. A good sports wash will remove it—but you will know if you have not gotten it all off if your legs are still burning in bed!

Though it's not exactly embrocation, some 'cross riders use a few drops of Olbas oil, either on a glove or collar or applied to the nostrils via cotton or a Q-tip, to ensure effective breathing at the start of a race. This, together with a decongestant rubbed on your chest, will clear the tubes for an explosive starting effort.

CHAPTER 3

Techniques and Tactics

Dismounting and Remounting

Watch a fast-moving string of top-class riders gracefully gliding on and off their bikes and jumping obstacles at speed; they make it look easy. Then watch riders at the other end of the scale attempting the same maneuvers; clearly, it's not as easy as it looks. Cyclocross takes skill, timing, and nerve, and the vital seconds and energy that can be saved by performing the skills well are crucial in the top echelons of the sport.

The frequent switches from cycling to running in 'cross, and vice versa, may have to be repeated five or even ten times a lap, depending on the nature of the course; multiply this by the ten laps of an average race, and suddenly you are performing a single skill up to a hundred times during a one-hour event. You must therefore be able to mount and dismount easily and automatically every time, even at a stressful point in a race—for instance, when you have just attacked and are trying to gain vital seconds.

The experience of racing over varied courses and conditions is invaluable in assessing which technique to use. But every technique must be learned during training—the race is no place to try out new ideas.

DISMOUNTING

You've ridden plenty of races, and you know how to get off your bike. But just think for a minute: Do you always do it the same way? Chances are you do, but is your technique right for every condition? The correct technique for a dismount at 20 miles an hour, performed in order to jump a low hurdle with an immediate remount, is considerably different from the technique required for a dismount halfway up an unrideable, muddy climb. So let's examine each condition you will encounter during a race.

Unrideable Climb

A common reason for dismounting is a hill that is too steep or slippery to ride. Before you dismount, select the gear you will want when you get back on your bike. If the climb is partly rideable but too slippery, you will already be in your bottom gear when you get off.

If the hill is too steep, approach it fast, with your hands either on the brake levers or on the tops of the bars. Swing your right leg over the back of the saddle, grab the top tube two or three inches in front of the seat post, and jump off, unclipping your left foot and putting as much weight as you can through your right arm onto the top tube.

If you are unsure about unclipping your foot from the pedal at this late stage, make it the first thing you do as you approach the dismount; unclip your foot and simply rest it on top of the pedal without clipping it back in, then continue as above.

As your feet hit the ground, start running and flick the bike up onto your shoulder by the top tube, or down tube, depending on your style.

Almost Rideable Climb

If the hill is almost rideable, then the time to dismount is just before you start to lose momentum. Don't carry on, riding more and more

A. With your hands on the brake levers, swing your right leg over the saddle and unclip your left foot from the pedal. Land on your right foot and start running.

B. As soon as you are into your stride, pick up your bike by your preferred method; here Tim picks up with the down tube. With the bike on your shoulder, slide your right arm under the down tube and grab the end of the left-hand dropped section of your bars. Note that Tim's left hand has not moved from the brake lever since he dismounted.

C. With this style of carrying, the weight of the bike is shared between your shoulder and your forearm. Simply slide the bike forward or backward on your shoulder to achieve a comfortable balance and an upright running style.

slowly, until you finally stop. You must maintain momentum at all times. A moving bike is far easier to pick up than a dead weight, so it is better to get off too soon and keep moving than to dismount too late and risk stopping altogether.

Forget about holding the top tube as you dismount; you will be traveling too slowly for this technique to work. Swing your right leg over the saddle, and as you push down on the left pedal, unclip it and jump off. Chances are that your hands will be firmly gripping the brake levers. Leave them there. Run the first few steps with your hands still on the levers until you get into your stride and back into your momentum, then pick the bike up by your preferred style, shoulder it, and carry on running.

Never run pushing your bike for more than five steps. If it is mud that forced you off your bike in the first place, it will suck at your tires, making pushing harder and clogging your wheels as you go. If it is the steepness of the hill that has forced you off, then it's so much easier to run with a bike on your shoulder than to try to push it up a steep incline. Still need convincing? Imagine your local supermarket is at the bottom of a long, steep hill. When you are walking back home with a heavy load of groceries, which is easier—carrying a bag in your hand at knee level or putting it in a backpack and carrying it high on your back?

When you have to run in cyclocross, always run with your bike on your shoulder.

Flat-Out Dismount

A flat-out dismount is usually performed to clear a hurdle quickly, with a fast remount to get straight back into your stride. This maneuver takes skill and nerve, and it can save or lose you the most time as well.

Your speed on the approach to the hurdle depends on your confidence. In training, start off slowly, and increase your speed until you feel sure you can approach the hurdle at race speed.

This is how it works. First, forget about shifting gears. Assume that the terrain after the obstacle is similar to the approach; with proper technique, you won't lose enough speed to need a gear shift. Your hand position should be the one you feel most confident with. The levers and the flat section on the tops of the bars are the favorite places for the hands during this type of approach. Perhaps it is best to reserve the tops until you have a very high level of confidence, as in this position

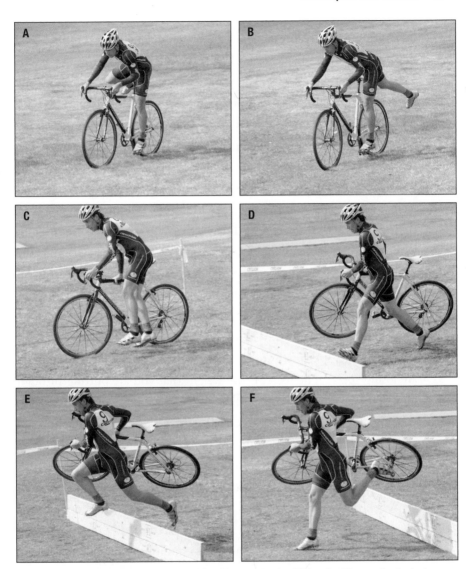

A. For a high-speed dismount for a set of hurdles, approach with hands either on the brake levers or, if you have top-mounted levers, on the tops. Unclip your right foot.

B. Swing your right leg over . . .

C. Grab the top tube with your right hand and put your weight through this arm. Unclip your left foot and if still some distance from the hurdle, "hover" in this position with both feet unclipped until you are two steps' distance away.

D. Land on your right foot, take one stride, then clear the hurdle with your right leg first.

E. Pick the bike up vertically so it goes back down on the ground straight. Alternatively, if you are moving too fast to do this, then flick it out slightly, as Tim has done.

F. Take one more stride after the hurdle to put the bike down and get your right hand back on the handlebars. Remount the bike on your next stride.

last-minute braking is out of the question and you are committed to jumping off at approach speed. So try the levers first.

Adjust your speed on the approach to give yourself plenty of time to swing your right leg over and get in position for the dismount. You won't slow down much, but you don't want to be hurried into making a mistake. Your right leg will be behind and slightly to the left of your left leg. Place your right hand on the top tube—again, three or four inches in front of the seat post—and lean your body back. With your weight on your right arm, unclip your left foot from its pedal and land right foot first on the ground. Lift the bike up with your right hand, while your left hand remains on the bars or brake lever, keeping the wheels straight so that when the bike hits the ground again it is under control. Clear the obstacle, put the bike back on the ground, your right hand back on the bars, and jump on.

Sounds easy, doesn't it? The tricky bit is taking as few steps as possible before and after the hurdle, because as soon as you are on foot, you are losing speed. The secret is the weight that you are putting through your right arm onto the top tube. The top people tend to jump off, take one full step, jump the obstacle on the next step, take one full step after the obstacle, and remount on the fourth. You may find that you need six or eight steps, but constant practice should give you the confidence to first try the dismount closer to the obstacle, and then faster.

When dismounting at speed, it's best to leave your left foot clipped in until the last part of the dismount. You can only do this with a high-quality pedal system and cleats in good condition, as they must release every time without fail; the consequences of a pedal that won't release as you approach a solid obstacle at 20 miles per hour are not good!

The alternative is to unclip your left foot first, before you swing your right leg over. You must then position your foot on the pedal in such a way that it will not clip in by mistake, and hope that there are no big bumps ahead that could make your foot bounce off the pedal. Personally, I prefer to keep my cleats in good shape and unclip at the last minute, but the choice is yours.

REMOUNTING

There are two different situations that call for remounting the bike: following a running section when the bike is on your shoulder and following an obstacle when the bike is just lifted up.

After a Running Section

Hold the bars with your left hand and the top tube with your right, then lift the bike off your shoulder and put it on the ground. Try to avoid dropping it too hard, as it can easily bounce out of control, wasting precious time.

When the bike is on the ground, get both hands on the bars in the position best suited to the next section of the circuit: the drops for a descent, the levers for a climb or any section out of the saddle, or the tops for a relatively smooth section. Then jump on with as few steps as possible.

For a remount with hands on the tops, use as wide a grip as possible. Also note that Tim is about to land on the saddle with the very top of the inside of his right thigh, which will give the appearance of "gliding" back onto the bike. The perfect remount style!

You should be able to jump into the saddle smoothly, clip into your pedals, and accelerate as if it were second nature, but problems can arise while clipping your feet in. If your pedals and shoes are right, then it is simply a question of practice, and this is the most important practice you can do. You should be able to get your feet clipped in first time, every time. No excuses!

After an Obstacle

Following the rapid dismount for a hurdle, it is most important to make sure that the bike is under control before you jump on. This means putting it down straight and getting both hands on the bars securely.

This is awkward to do flat-out while trying to take only two steps before remounting, so practice slowly and build up speed, as with dismounting. There are two ways to get your bike over the hurdle as

The most common hand position for a remount is on the brake levers. This makes immediate, out-of-the-saddle, fast accelerations to get back up to speed more natural.

Remount on the drops if you have an immediate descent ahead of you.

your feet are doing their thing; ideally you should lift the bike up into the air by bending your arms at the elbow. Keep the bike as vertically straight as possible so that it will go back onto the ground straight. When you're getting faster, or when you're traveling too fast to pick up the bike quickly enough, you may tend to flick the bike outward (as if you were trying to show a spectator on the right-hand side of the course the bottom of your wheels). This is okay, but you must make sure the bike is back on the ground in a vertical plane before you jump back on; otherwise you'll veer off to whichever side the bike is leaning. Good if you know the spectators you are heading for, bad if you don't!

Running with the Bike

How you run—and more importantly, how you carry your bike—will significantly affect your ability to breathe properly and keep your upper body relaxed.

It's quite difficult to describe an effective style for running with a bike on your shoulder, but when I was picking the brains of some of the Dutch guys to find out how they train, they described a good running style as "running like a woman." When I pressed for more information, one of them said, "You know . . . swinging your spare arm and using your whole body to run, like women do!" What these top riders had in mind can be seen in the running style of, say, Richard Groenendaal, a very fast and efficient runner. Though the way they described it may sound a bit sexist, the running style itself is very effective.

This is the reason you should include at least a little running in your training schedule. Sooner or later running in deep mud will be inevitable!

Carrying the bike with your arm around the front of the head tube automatically pushes your bike farther back on your shoulder and gives you an upright running style, which in turn aids breathing and means you are looking ahead at the course. It also gives better exposure to the sponsor's branding on your chest!

For a taller guy like Ryan Trebon, carrying his bike with his arm under the down tube means he has to stoop slightly. Try both styles and go with the most comfortable for your running style.

There are two main techniques for carrying the bike; both give you a nice upright style, and the choice between the two will be governed by your build. In the first, the arm goes around the front of the head tube and the hand grasps the brake lever. This technique is best suited to tall riders. In the second, the arm goes under the down tube, which then rests in the bend of the arm, and the hand grasps the dropped part of the bar. This style works best for shorter riders.

Avoid any style that pushes the weight of the bike forward and down with the corner of the top tube or seat tube resting on your shoulder. This method tends to make you lean forward, which restricts your breathing and forces you to lift your head awkwardly to see where you are going.

While carrying the bike, try to run as upright as possible on the flat, but lean forward slightly into any hills you have to climb. On steep hills, some riders like to push their left thigh with the left hand to give it a bit of help. Occasionally, you may have to run downhill if the descent is unrideable or is followed by an immediate return up a climb, and occasionally you might have to run a descent on the early laps of a race, as traffic may not allow you to ride a section straight after it. It becomes faster to stay off the bike and run the whole section. For the descent, lean back slightly into the slope and use your free arm for balance. It is important to watch where you are putting your feet, especially if the descent is unrideable because of too many rocks or roots, since falls while running can easily cause injury.

Unless the running section is particularly long (most are fairly short sections over hurdles or up banks), the effect should be a fast burst, not a gentle jog. When running uphill, especially in sand or mud, short, fast steps will mean a better grip; if you overstretch, you have more chance of slipping. On the flat, however, you can stride out.

Decide during your warm-up whether to use studs, spikes, or nothing at all in the front of your shoes. Your decision should be based on the ground conditions you will encounter when you have to dismount and cover ground on foot. Generally, use studs when the mud is deep, not just surface "slime" on hard ground, and spikes on a layer of surface slime to penetrate the top layer and grip the hard ground below. Spikes also work well on hard snow or ice. If there is anything slippery, either on dismount or on an uphill run, you would probably benefit from something in the front of your shoe, but if either you do not need to dismount or the ground is dry and firm, then leave the studs and spikes off. (Always put a "blank" in the stud/spike holes to cover the threads so they won't become damaged or full of dirt. Blanks usually come with the shoes; they are simply flat-headed covers that pro-tect the threads.) As a rule, avoid spikes if you have to dismount on concrete or rocks, as they will be too slippery. If in doubt, do a warm-up lap experimenting with studs or spikes to see what works best.

Picking Up the Bike

There are two possible methods of picking up your bike, and the one you will use depends on your carrying style. The best, as it's the fastest and you don't have to bend down to do it, is to pick up using the top tube.

This should be done with the hand on the top of the top tube (knuckles facing upward), not underneath the top tube (palm facing

Picking the bike up with the top tube.

Picking the bike up with the down tube.

upward). The technique involves a short, sharp flick of the bike, which is more easily achieved with the hand from the top; this is also the place your hand will naturally be after the majority of dismounts. This method is the best one to use if you carry the bike with your arm around the head tube. But if you carry the bike with your arm under the down tube, you might prefer to pick it up with the down tube, as it will then be easier to slide your arm under as you start to run.

To put the bike down off your shoulder, hold the bars with your left hand and take it off your shoulder with your right hand on the top tube. Either slide the top tube down your arm onto your hand and then onto the ground or keep hold of the top tube as you initially take it from your shoulder.

Incidentally, when changing bikes, don't throw your bike from your shoulder onto the ground, as you can easily bend handlebars and shifters this way. Take it off as described, and when it is on the ground, let go or give it to someone.

Cornering

Cornering in 'cross is very similar to cornering on roads, but as you may be encountering slippery surfaces, it is important not to turn the bars excessively or lean too much. You also have to turn much tighter corners than you would ever find on the road, and at much slower speeds. You must eliminate as much of the corner as possible by approaching along the correct line so as to cross the apex of the bend with a line that is as nearly straight as possible. You must be prepared to feel the bike moving under you, especially in mud or snow, but only experience will tell you how much movement is safe or when you will slide off.

You must reduce your speed on the approach to a corner so you are not trying to adjust your speed as you go into it or when you actually are in the corner. It is best in general to keep off the brakes while in the midst of cornering. As with any rule, there are exceptions to this one, however. As a race proceeds or as a succession of races affects the surface during the day, the apex might become very slippery. In this case, look for grip (usually grass) around the outside of the corner. Because there is grip, and because it is a wider arc around the corner, you will be able to continue pedaling around it, and although it's farther, it's probably faster.

There are three critical factors that affect cornering. First, where you look is where you go. Concentrate on looking at the exit of the corner, not the apex, and certainly not the tree on the outside edge of the tape just after the apex, as that is exactly where you will be drawn. Look at photos or footage of the top riders cornering and check their head and eye position; the majority have their heads up or at least level, and their eyes are looking forward, not down. Second, you must remain relaxed and "loose." If your upper body and arms stiffen up, the effect is to keep your head down so you're not looking at your exit, which messes up your line. In addition, if you are tense you cannot react quickly to a slip of wheels. Third, tire pressure is everything! If you appear to be sliding when others have grip, then you've got your tires too hard, pure and simple.

A great example of concentration while cornering. Sven Nys is perfectly balanced and is looking at the exit from the corner in this high-speed shot.

Use your front brake, or a combination of both brakes, when approaching a corner, but take the corner itself without brakes to keep the bike under control. Change your line accordingly to avoid cornering on roots or rocks or any slippery surface, as the bike will move a lot more. Your outside leg should be straight with a lot of weight going through it, and your inside leg bent with the knee pointing slightly outward.

During 'cross races you will encounter an enormous variety of conditions, each requiring a slightly different approach. Only by encountering them all will you know how the bike responds and how you can control it. Confidence in your bike-handling ability and correct tire pressures can make all the difference in the world, and if someone else can get around a corner fast, there is no reason why you can't. It's just a question of practice and nerve. You will only discover your limitations by falling off a few times—if you train well, most of these falls can take place during training. When you do fall, 99 percent of the time you will not hurt yourself, as you will simply slide.

While you are watching footage of the 'cross stars, check out how much more they continue to pedal around slow corners than you do. A wheel that is being "driven" around through pressure on the pedals will grip better than a freewheeling wheel at very slow speeds. Experience, exceptional balance, and confidence don't hurt either.

Once in a while you'll encounter hairpin corners where the course changes direction 180 degrees. These turns seem to require an almost dead stop to negotiate. In these situations, try using the inside marking post (if it is secure) as something to grab hold of to swing you around the corner.

For very slow, tight turns on deep or slippery mud, you may simply grab the central marking post and swing yourself around on it.

This shot shows perfectly the need to be able to attack climbs out of the saddle. Short, sharp, explosive turns of speed are a feature of the best 'cross riders, and the best way to achieve this is out of the saddle.

Finally, we all know the worst surface for cornering is ice. On icy surfaces, keep the bike in as straight a line as possible, and avoid any sharp movements or unnecessary braking.

Climbing

Most climbing in 'cross is done out of the saddle with the hands on the brake levers. The drops should never be used for climbing, as you need your upper body to be as straight as possible to assist with breathing—which is vital on a climb.

The compromise between traction on the climb and speed is one of the biggest problems a cyclocross rider faces. On long, slippery climbs off-road, you must ride slightly out of the saddle with your weight as far back as possible, unlike on the road, where you tend to be over the handlebars with relatively straight arms. In this position, there is significant strain on your forearms and shoulders, and it is not unusual for these parts of the body to tire the quickest. You cannot afford to sway the bike beneath you as you do on the road; the bike must be kept steady in a straight line.

On shorter climbs, whether you make it up—and if you do, how fast you do it—is determined by your approach speed. You need as much speed as you can get as you hit the climb so that you can coast up it without having to pedal too much. Do not try to approach the climb at a normal speed, change to your lowest gear, and pedal up it—you will not make it to the top. The lower the gear you use, the less traction you will have, and wheel spin will bring you to a halt. Using big gears and approaching climbs at speed takes a lot of strength, but this is the best attribute a 'cross rider can have.

Having good traction often comes down to having the correct tires at the correct pressure. As with going around corners, in climbs most people have their tires pumped up too hard, which seriously reduces grip. Let some air out—you will find it helps a lot.

Descending

A good descender needs both nerve and skill. The skills and techniques can be learned and practiced, and although nerve is an in-built characteristic, if something is practiced to the point where confidence grows, then nerve need not be a limiting factor.

The biggest mistake a beginner can make when descending is to go too slowly. It is actually easier to go faster, as you can ride over things at speed that throw you off balance when you are going more slowly.

There are a number of points to remember while descending. Avoid too much use of the front brake, as it impairs steering. Also,

Perfect descending technique: relaxed but balanced, cranks level, off the back of the saddle, and with eyes looking straight ahead. No wonder Katie Compton is a World Championship medalist!

heavy braking with the back usually locks your wheel. This is okay if it is controlled, but you can easily lose control if your wheel is sliding and you have to corner.

Try to descend with your hands on the dropped part of your handlebars, as they will be able to reach the brake levers more easily while gripping the bars for security. This position also gives you a better distribution of weight. Ease yourself slightly off the saddle, and keep your weight back, balancing the saddle between your thighs. Let your legs absorb the shocks.

Do not be afraid to unclip a foot on corners or cambers during a descent. If the bike starts to slide, you can dab with your foot and keep yourself upright. If you descend with one foot out, keep the leg that is

Don't be afraid to take a foot out while descending. It automatically puts your weight farther back and on a camber it weights the downslope side of the bike, which improves traction. Plus it's easy to dab your foot to make corrections if you start to slide. It's also great for confidence. As long as you are adept at getting your foot back on your pedal, you will not lose any time using this technique.

still in the pedal straight with a lot of weight through it, and use your free leg to balance with. As long as you can clip your foot back in the pedal quickly, you will lose absolutely no time descending with a foot out of the pedal. The added security can help you avoid crashes while giving you confidence to descend faster than you would otherwise.

Sort out your lines down the hills during your warm-up. You need to take the straightest line possible, which may mean descending across the hill to ensure a good line for the next part of the circuit. If you are a confident descender, attacking just before a descent is an excellent way to get a gap. Sizable differences can appear on descents between the good and the not-so-good, and this is where the race can be won or lost.

Bunny-Hopping

Bunny-hopping hurdles has come almost full circle over the past couple of decades. In the early 1980s, riders rarely bothered to try jumping hurdles on their bikes. Then, Danny De Bie won a World Championship title in 1987 because he could ride some planks and the subsequent climbs after them while his opponents were forced to dismount. Even then, he wasn't bunny-hopping as such; he was riding the planks one wheel at a time, actually quite slowly, but he was still on board his bike and had momentum for the climbs. Then the likes of Sven Nys and Bart Wellens started riding fast hurdles at speed with both wheels off the ground. This was real bunny-hopping, and everyone was trying to learn a new technique to avoid getting left behind. Along with the UCI's reform of the sport in 2004, however, came some changes to rules and regulations that affected the new technique. Now, only one set of hurdles per lap is allowed, and there has to be a maximum distance of 4 meters between hurdles. This is not quite enough distance to get the second one right in a bunny hop (unless your name is Nys!). So now, in Europe at least, it's actually quite rare to see anyone attempting to jump hurdles if he or she is in a traditional pair, as the risk is very high for not so much gain.

To bunny-hop obstacles during a race, you must be absolutely certain that you can do it every single time. Nine times out of ten is no good, because the one time you don't make it will cost you more time than you gained on all the previous nine put together. You also risk doing serious damage to yourself and your bike. If any technique needs rigorous practice during training to get it perfect, this is the one.

There are two types of bunny hops: the kind where you clear the obstacle at speed with both wheels in the air, and the slower technique used for higher obstacles where you take the obstacle one wheel at a time. The latter is only useful if you can ride a subsequent section of the circuit faster by staying on your bike—for example, when a rideable climb is preceded by an obstacle. Otherwise, it is normally faster to dismount at speed and jump the obstacle.

Let's examine the techniques required for both methods. For a clear bunny hop, first make sure your pedals are in good shape, with adequate spring tension to keep your foot in place, as it is by pulling up with hands and feet that you get the bike in the air. Pulling a foot out of its pedal during such a move can have some nasty consequences! Your hands may be either on the tops or on the brake levers, but never on the drops, as that messes up your weight distribution. The tops are good for getting lots of pull, but not so good if you need to control your speed at the last moment, unless you have the "extra" set of brake levers.

Your position should be fairly upright; you should be out of the saddle with the cranks level and your weight directly over the pedals. Pull up your front wheel first, then shift your weight forward and pull up on the pedals, and your rear wheel will simply follow the front. Do not try to lift both wheels simultaneously. But do try to ensure that your takeoff is straight and the bike level so that your landing is the same—otherwise, you will be out of control when your wheels touch the ground.

To practice this move in training, place something light—a small branch, a wooden pole, or a curtain rod—on two stacks of bricks.

Not too many riders can bunny-hop hurdles, and there are few opportunities when it is faster to do it, but here Adam McGrath shows the technique to use.

Start low, and then gradually add bricks to increase the height. If you hit the bar it will simply fall off, so you should be able to avoid crashes or damage to your wheels.

For riding over an obstacle too high to clear with both wheels, the best place for the hands is on the brake levers. Lift the front wheel up with your weight back; as it lands, throw your weight forward and help the back wheel over by pulling up on the pedals.

There is a fine line between going fast enough to keep your momentum and get your cranks and back wheel over, and going too fast to get the rear wheel up, with the result that it hits the obstacle too hard and throws you over the bars. Also, if you try to hit the obstacle too slowly, you will find yourself with a wheel on both sides of it and unable to move, probably with a bent chainring or rear wheel as well.

Techniques for Specific Course Conditions

CAMBERS

If the course is routed across a slope, you will have to contend with the problem of sliding downward when you want to travel straight across. If the camber is severe, you will not be able to pedal, as the uphill pedal will catch on the ground. The best method of dealing with this situation is to get as much speed up as possible before you reach the camber to allow you to freewheel across the offending section.

Going straight across without succumbing to the tendency to drop down is a matter of weight distribution, with as much weight as possible on the downslope pedal. If the camber is severe, you may need to shift some body weight to assist you. Unless you can get across without any problems, take your uphill foot out of the pedal and leave your leg out; this automatically puts all your weight onto the correct pedal, and if the bike starts to slide you will be able to push yourself back upright quickly before you fall off. The aim is to stay as high as possible on cambers. If you slip to the bottom, unless the circuit then turns down the hill, you will have big problems getting back up without dismounting.

If you need to dismount on a camber, you will encounter a number of difficulties that require some skill to overcome. If you have to get off on the uphill side, you cannot put your pedal down in its usual place, as it will catch on the ground. So you must jump as the pedal is on its way down. If you have to jump off on the downhill side, you will land with your feet a lot lower than the bike, and it will not be easy to get it on your shoulder.

On cambers, stay as upright as possible with as much weight as you can get on your downslope pedal; unclipping the upslope foot helps. Focusing on where you want to go also stops you from naturally heading downhill, as Dan Alexander shows here as he takes to the bushes.

MUD

Just as Eskimos have a hundred different words for snow, so 'cross cyclists should have a varied vocabulary to describe the different types of mud they encounter. Mud in one type of soil or ecosystem is always a little different from mud in another type, and the specific type of mud affects the bike and your riding technique.

Slippery, wet, sticky clay; mud with grass, with leaves, on rocks, on roots—the list is endless. But all types of mud have one thing in common: They slow the bike down. It is amazing just what depths of mud can be ridden through. But a lot of it comes down to momentum—a rider's best friend—and letting the bike go where it wants.

A "light" riding style is needed to get through mud: That means hands on the tops, a gear that won't be a struggle to maintain should you encounter a particularly bad section, and enough confidence to let the bike make its own line. The right style is neither in the saddle nor standing on the pedals, but halfway between the two, lifting yourself very slightly off the seat to get more power while maintaining traction.

Again, tire pressure is also vital. Soft tires provide much better grip in muddy conditions. The only excuse for hard tires is when the circuit is rocky or has sections through hard, icy ruts that cause compression punctures (pinch-flats). The best tire treads for mud are either the chevron/arrow, as found on the Challenge or Dugast Typhoon, or, for the particularly gloopy days, a mud-specific tread, as found on a Dugast Rhino or Michelin Mud2.

The biggest problem with mud is that it clogs up your bike. A nice, light, 18-pound bike can double in weight in a couple of laps, especially if the mud is mixed in with grass, which grinds gears to a halt and fouls the wheels. Change bikes regularly in muddy races; if you can't change bikes for some reason, then run the really bad bits, and as you are running, try to scrape off the worst of the mud. If there are any particularly wet sections on the circuit, riding through these can also help clean your wheels and frame.

SAND

Sand is the hallmark of a Dutch 'cross race, and it is very awkward stuff to race in. On the bike, it slows you down very quickly indeed, and it's nearly impossible to steer a course through. On foot, carrying your bike, you feel like you are going nowhere fast, particularly uphill.

When approaching sand on the bike, you should hold the bars firmly on the tops with an upright style and attempt to hit the sandy area fast in a big gear and churn your way through it. The bike will make its own mind up which way to go, so you must just hold on and keep pedaling, because as soon as you start to freewheel you will simply stop.

Sand is not a standard obstacle for road sprint superstar
Fred Rodriguez.

If the section is short and as quick to run, then do it. Sand is a
complete wrecker of equipment; ten laps through a 50-meter stretch
are enough to necessitate a new chain and sprockets, together with a
total strip-down of the rest of the bike. It gets everywhere, and if not
removed, will destroy bearings before you know it.

If you find yourself racing in sand a lot (maybe when you relocate
to the Netherlands!), then fit fat tires to your wheels. A minimum of
a 32 mm tire, either clincher or tubular, is required, but 34 mm
would be significantly better. Tread design does not have much ef-

fect in sand, but many riders encountering a sandy course use a file tread front and rear. This type of tread will be faster on any road sections and better for sections of hard-packed sand, where a more aggressive tread would break through the surface. It's better to ride on top of sand whenever possible. Sandy courses are definitely the place to break out the deep-rim wheels, which cut through the sand. These will work significantly better than low rims and will provide more steering control.

To run effectively in sand, a style similar to a duck waddling is best. This "waddling" should be in short, fast strides. During training before the World Championships in Koksijde, Belgian coach Eric De Vlaeminck told his riders to put their feet in the footprints of the people in front of them. This is good advice; in a footprint, the sand is already compressed, and it requires less effort to run on compressed sand.

ICE

Ice is very difficult stuff to race on. Riders from countries where there is a lot of ice and snow during the 'cross season, such as Switzerland, Slovakia, and the Czech Republic, have a great advantage over riders from countries with more temperate climates, who rarely encounter it for more than a couple of races each year.

It takes skill to ride on ice, but it also takes confidence. In fact, lack of confidence is the biggest problem to overcome on ice. As soon as you start to get nervous, it becomes very hard to stay upright. You must stay on top of it all the time and be positive. A big advantage on an icy circuit is the ability to roll a big gear with very little upper body movement.

A file-tread tire at the front is helpful on the ice; on the back, use either a file-tread tire, if you don't need grip anywhere, or a chevron. Definitely do not use big studs on either the front or the rear. Also, fat tires—34 mm—are an advantage. The tire pressure should be as low

The ability to ride on ice was a prime requisite at the World Championships in St. Wendel, Germany, where frozen conditions made the surface treacherous.

as you dare use, unless any of the circuit is sharply rutted, in which case you may need a bit more pressure to avoid pinch-flats.

Braking on ice is very tricky. Never brake hard or suddenly—always use gradual braking, and try to avoid locking up your rear wheel, as it will simply slide away from you.

Shoe grip for running on ice is difficult to achieve. Studs simply slide, so try spikes, which will provide more grip on hard ice.

SNOW

Fresh snow is totally different from ice and calls for different techniques and cautions. Resembling mud if it is deep, snow is not as slippery to ride on, and you can afford to use tires with more grip. But you can keep a file tread on the front if you have one available, as it will allow for better steering. The biggest problem with snow is braking in it, as it coats both rims and brake pads. This means braking has little effect until the snow has worn off, so extra care must be taken on descents.

But bear in mind that when snow becomes compacted after a number of laps, it takes on all the characteristics of ice. The advice in the section above should be heeded in these conditions. Alternatively, a snowy circuit on a warm day can become a mud bath by the end of the race as the thaw kicks in while races progress. Keep your eyes open as conditions change, and particularly look out for new lines that develop.

Although your bike will appear clean, you still must change bikes regularly in the snow. The sprockets quickly become full of snow, causing the gears to jump, and the chain will require lubing more often.

ROCKS AND ROOTS

Wherever possible, both rocks and roots should be avoided if an alternative line can be found around them. Rocks are particularly troublesome—the main problem with them is that they can cause punctures. Any course with rocky sections should be ridden with harder tires, around 4 bars (58 psi).

Wooded courses always contain numerous roots, which become unearthed as the race progresses. They can be very tough obstacles, as you get absolutely no grip when riding along them or crossing them. Try to avoid riding your front wheel over them unless they are flat, and don't attempt to turn, as this will simply bring you down. Keep the weight on your bars light, and if possible pull your front wheel up and over to clear them. The rear wheel will invariably slide, too, so attempt the same lifting maneuver with the rear and try to bunny-hop over it, or at the least unweight it a little. Always be on the lookout for alternative lines as they appear—and they will on each lap—as soil that is soft enough to expose a root in the first place will erode quickly with a few dozen bikes churning over it every six minutes.

Tire pressures have relatively little effect on roots, although a harder tire will generally slide more, so consider the rest of the terrain before choosing your tire pressures. Don't make a decision based solely on the roots.

CHAPTER 4

Training Basics

A cyclocross race, depending on your age or category, is a 40- to 60-minute effort. For the majority of competitors, the effort is maximal for the entire race, but there are also dramatic changes in pace. Difficult stretches of terrain, uphill efforts, and obstacles such as hurdles where you must dismount and carry your bike alternate with efforts to reach and maintain maximum speed. With respect to fitness and effort and the requirement to ride at your threshold, it is similar to a 40-kilometer time trial or a criterium. Add into the equation the technical aspects of the race—the hurdling, the cornering, the start, and the occasional need to cover sections of the course on foot—and you have, in a nutshell, the bases that you need to cover in training.

What cannot be avoided, and what you must have to maximize the genes your parents so kindly handed down to you, is a platform of base building and basic conditioning to as high a level as you can achieve. Quite simply, the conditioning you have will dictate both your level of fitness and the effect that specific training, such as intervals and high-zone work, will have on your fitness. The peak has to be supported by the base; you might be able to achieve a high peak for a while in 'cross by hammering interval sessions three times a week, but with no real base the peak will crumble very fast.

As for training principles, there are a zillion books and Web sites dedicated to the facts and the myths about training, and every coach has his or her own principles and ideas, but every one of these approaches is slightly different from the next. There are not only whole chapters but whole books out there covering the topics I will skim over in a few sentences as I attempt to convey the bigger picture of 'cross training. Browse through the "Recommended Reading" section at the end of this book for titles and Web sites that will expand on the subjects that interest you.

There are two simple principles that are indisputable if you want to train to fulfill your potential in cyclocross. First, there is no substitute for hard work. Cycling is a sport where results flow from effort; in other words, you get out of it what you put into it in terms of both time and effort. Second, there is no shortcut. You simply have to spend time in the saddle. You are a bike rider, so ride it!

Finally, it is important to realize that everyone is different. Although principles of training apply in a broad physiological sense to everybody, the circumstances under which you carry out your training, as well as your lifestyle, your genetic makeup, and your individual health considerations, will dictate how well certain principles work. You are not a lab rat.

Training Zones

In the following sections, I will refer to six different "zones" of training to simplify training routines. These six numbered zones (plus a "recovery" zone that sits under Zone 1) are simply extensions of the original four that were devised in the 1990s, but with a distinct zone for each type of training (as opposed to an "upper" or "lower" level within a zone, a shortcoming of the old system). The zones have been established from the results of laboratory exercise tests covering every level of intensity and duration. Structuring your training becomes very simple when you use these zones as guideposts.

You can base this training in terms of heart rate (HR) or power (watts, or W) to get a clearer picture of how hard you are really working in a session. If you don't have a heart rate monitor or power meter (for example, the SRM crank, the Powertap hub, and the Ergomo bracket) and cannot afford to buy one, it's not the end of the world. See if you can borrow a monitor and/or meter, as it's quite possible to get a feel for certain heart rates, and how your body is functioning at those heart rates, by simply using them for a short time. For example, can you hold a conversation? Does it feel like race pace? After a while, you will be able to gauge your efforts pretty accurately even when you don't have the monitor.

First, you need to determine your maximum HR, as the training zones are based on it. There are two ways to do this. One is to book yourself for a ramp test in a local lab, which might be at a university, sports clinic, cycling federation office, or regional sports institute. If you have a coach, he or she might have the capability to do this for you. But you can measure your own maximum heart rate quite easily yourself. After a few days of rest or easy, light training, simply warm up fully and then ride up a hill, gradually increasing your effort until you are giving it absolutely maximum effort over the top. Record your heart rate during the effort, or, if your heart rate monitor just displays and doesn't record, then as you see stars from the effort, try to focus on the number it gives you as you max out at the top of your hill. If you are fresh for this test and confident that you couldn't have tried any harder, this will be your maximum heart rate. Record this figure, and then use Table 4.1 to find your zones of training.

Using the chart is easy. To find out what a Zone 1 effort would be for you, for example, find your max HR in the left-hand column. Say it's 190. Then when you are training in Zone 1, your heart rate will be 114 to 123. During a recovery ride (REC), your heart rate should go no higher than 113. And so on. Remember to retest your max HR every so often, as gains in fitness will alter it and you can be a zone "out" if you don't keep track of your progress. Max HR will also decrease with age, so keep an eye on the figures you are getting and adjust accordingly.

TABLE 4.1 Zones Based on Max Heart Rate

MAX HR	RECOV.	Z1	Z2	Z3	Z4	Z5	Z6
180	107 max	108–116	117–134	135–147	148–159	160–168	169–180
182	108 max	109–117	118–136	137–148	149–161	162–170	171–182
184	109 max	110–119	120–137	138–150	151–163	164–172	173–184
186	111 max	112–120	121–139	140–152	153–165	166–174	175–186
188	112 max	113–121	122–140	141–153	154–166	167–176	177–188
190	113 max	114–123	124–142	143–155	156–168	169–178	179–190
192	114 max	115–124	125–143	144–156	157–170	171–179	180–192
194	115 max	116–125	126–145	146–158	159–172	173–181	182–194
196	117 max	118–126	127–146	147–160	161–173	174–183	184–196
198	118 max	119–128	129–148	149–161	162–175	176–185	186–198
200	119 max	120–129	130–149	150–163	164–177	178–187	188–200
202	120 max	121–130	131–151	152–165	166–179	180–189	190–202
204	121 max	122–132	133–152	153–166	167–181	182–191	192–204
206	123 max	124–133	134–154	155–168	169–182	183–193	194–206
208	124 max	125–134	135–155	156–170	171–184	185–195	196–208
210	125 max	126–136	137–157	158–171	172–186	187–196	197–210

TRAINING ZONES

The zones themselves can be used for different training goals and can be used in different combinations throughout a training block, month, or season. They are as follows:

- **Recovery**

  Easy riding for up to 1 hour. Not a training session, per se, but to aid in recovery.

- **Zone 1: Base Endurance 1**

  Long, steady riding for up to 6 hours in duration. For development of economy and efficiency with very high-volume, low-stress work. Very long sessions improve the combustion and storage of fats.

(continues)

Combine with Zone 2 for practical, unstructured, low-stress rides. Best performed in small groups. Attempt to maintain a constant pace. Correct carbohydrate feeding is important both during and immediately after the session.

Frequency: One or two sessions per week.

- **Zone 2: Base Endurance 2**

Riding at a moderate, steady pace for up to 4 hours in duration. For development of economy and efficiency using high-volume, moderate-stress work. This zone is an important intensity for establishing a firm base for all riders. Combine it with Zone 1 for practical, unstructured, low-stress rides. Zone 2 trains a fair proportion of the muscle fibers to use a mixture of carbohydrate and fat and provides moderate training of the oxygen-transport system. Best performed in small groups. Attempt to maintain a constant pace. Correct carbohydrate feeding is important both during and immediately after the session.

Frequency: Two or three sessions per week.

- **Zone 3: Intensive Endurance 1**

Hard effort of up to 90 minutes in duration. For development of aerobic capacity and endurance, with moderate-volume work at a controlled intensity. Ideally done alone or in a small group to ensure you stay in zone. Possible (but boring) on an indoor trainer for up to 1 hour in bad weather. "Modules" can be incorporated into Zone 1 or 2 rides to increase intensity while maintaining volume.

Frequency: Two sessions per week.

- **Zone 4: Intensive Endurance 2**

Hard efforts of up to 60 minutes in duration. Typical "mean" intensity of most road races. Useful for tapering and as preparation for simulating race pace. Sessions should be ended when the effort starts to tell.

Frequency: One or two sessions per week.

(continues)

- **Zone 5: Maximum Endurance 1**

  Intensive effort of up to 20 minutes in duration, or intervals. For raising of anaerobic threshold, improvement of lactate clearance, and adaptation to race speed. Zone 5 sessions should be done alone. There are three different situations where you would use a Zone 5 effort: (1) as a specific road or "turbo" session, (2) for controlled periods within a shortened Zone 1 or 2 session, or (3) in a 10- or 25-mile time trial.

  Frequency: One session per week.

- **Zone 6: Maximum Endurance 2**

  Maximal effort, including short intervals of 10 to 30 seconds, medium intervals of 45 to 60 seconds, and long intervals of 90 seconds to 3 minutes. The rest intervals should be long enough to recover from the effort. This is high-intensity interval training to increase maximum power and improve lactate production or clearance. Ideally, it is best done on hills or on an indoor trainer. It should be done only when completely recovered from previous work. Heart rates are not the best guide for this type of training. The intensity should be such that the effort can be held just to the end of the interval. Use heart rate for feedback, but be in tune with how your body is feeling to work at this level. Your breathing will be very rapid and uncomfortable, and it should feel like you are doing something very physically and psychologically demanding.

  Frequency: One session per week.

Since each zone description above indicates how many times a week you should perform a particular type of session, drawing up a training plan should be simple. You can change the frequency of various sessions depending on what stage of your year or season plan you find yourself in. For instance, during a conditioning phase, you would want to increase the number of Zone 1 and 2 workouts while reducing or removing entirely any sessions at above Zone 4. The frequency given for any particular zone indicates the maximum number of times that session should ideally be included within a weekly plan for maximum effect. However, you must decide for yourself how much time you are prepared to devote to training. Then you can work out your plan, either by yourself or with the help of a coach.

As most people cannot train full-time and must fit in training and racing around work and family commitments, it can be difficult to figure out how to fit in all these sessions and train in your various zones appropriately. Next, we shall take a look at how that can be done.

Training on a Workday

Every racer would love to be able to train and rest full-time, but unless you are prepared to sacrifice everything in pursuit of your sport, the chances are that you will be working. And unless you are in a position to work shifts or "flextime," you will also have to contend with doing most of your training in the dark. But if you are keen to improve and dedicated in your approach, these time constraints—and the discomforts of training in winter weather—must be overcome.

The first thing you must do is work out the time you have available to train, taking work and other commitments into consideration. Circumstances will dictate how to set up a training schedule. A single person may be able to devote more time to training than someone with a family, for instance, and those who can commute by bike to work, and who have access to changing and shower facilities once they get there, will have more training time available than someone who has a long commute by car.

The time you have available in an evening will probably not amount to much more than 60 to 90 minutes, but this is as much as is required for one session. Take a look at the rest of your day. Is it possible to fit in a 15-minute run before work, or a short session on an indoor trainer or a gym workout in your lunch hour? If the answer is yes, then suddenly you have the ability to fit in a three-session day every now and then—total time 2 to 2.5 hours—which is just fine.

If you are limited to the hour at the end of the day, it's not the end of the world—you will simply have to go for quality instead of quantity. Provided you can build up a reasonable base of longer rides during the longer evenings in the summer and over the weekends, you will have the basis of a good regime for cyclocross racing.

If time is tight or the weather is so bad that you cannot face going out on the bike, then you have two alternatives: Hop on the indoor trainer for a session or go for a run. Running is easier to fit in than riding and may seem like less of a chore in very bad weather (although you should never venture out when it's icy or foggy, as it becomes too dangerous). On such days, stick to the indoor trainer or use your circuit of stretching, core, and indoor exercises.

As with all training, it should be progressive, with gradual increases in quality as the season progresses and the bigger races approach. It's important to have periods of rest to recover mentally from the pressures of training hard and to keep a careful check on your health; be alert for any hints your body may give you that you may be doing too much too soon. It will also be a good idea mid-season to miss the occasional weekend of racing to have a mini weekend "training camp" instead. At this time, you can top off your endurance conditioning with some back-to-back long road rides like the ones that are possible during the summer.

Training Cycles and Phases

For your training, work in cycles of three or four weeks followed by an easier week. With each cycle, the workouts should become progressively harder. Following a gradual buildup over the summer, and then beginning in September with your first training cycle, you will go through four or five cycles before the end of the season in February.

For example, let's assume you can fit in two sessions a day totaling 90 minutes, and that you work during the day. For the five cycles of the season, you could follow a training schedule like the one in Table 4.2.

TRAINING DETAILS

Each phase of training should include three weeks of training followed by one week of rest. Try to train on four of the weekdays, as described in Table 4.2, and continue with stretching and core work. The purpose of the rest week is to recover from the previous three weeks and to prepare mentally for the increased efforts of the next phase. Do not force yourself to train during this week. If the weather is bad, or you do not feel like going out, take a break. The rest week schedule should remain the same for each phase, while the training schedule will gradually become more demanding.

Don't forget to record your resting heart rate each morning before you get up, and record your weight each week. This will form an important part of your training diary (see "Keeping a Training Diary" later in this chapter). Over a period of time, this information will help you understand how your body works and how it copes with training loads. Besides the workouts in the schedule, add in evening stretching and core work where possible.

In Phases 4 and 5, Tuesday morning run intervals should be done on an incline, if possible. Run 100 meters uphill and jog down to recover. The bicycle sprints in Phases 4 and 5 can be accelerations out of corners or up hills.

TABLE 4.2 Sample Season Training Plan

Phase 1: September

WEEKS 1–3

	Monday	Tuesday	Wednesday	Thursday
A.M.	20-min. trail run, steady	20-min. trail run, steady	20-min. trail run, steady	20-min. trail run, steady
P.M.	1-hr. road ride, Z2 or Z3	1-hr. road ride, Z2 or Z3	1-hr. road ride, Z2 or Z3	1-hr. road ride, Z2 or Z3

WEEK 4 (Recovery week is the same for each phase.)

Monday	Tuesday	Wednesday	Thursday
1-hr. ride, Z1	20-min. run	1-hr. ride, Z1	20-min. run

Phase 2: October

	Monday	Tuesday	Wednesday	Thursday
A.M.	1-hr. road ride, Z1	20-min. run	20-min. run	20-min. run
P.M.		1-hr. road ride, Z3	1-hr. ride warm-up 30 min., Z4 cool-down	1-hr. road ride, Z3

Phase 3: November

	Monday	Tuesday	Wednesday	Thursday
A.M.	1-hr. road ride, Z2	25-min. run	30-min. trainer 5-min. warm-up 5 x 30 sec., Z6 2-min. recovery 10-min. cool-down	20-min. run
P.M.		1-hr. road ride, Z3	1-hr. road ride, Z2	1-hr. ride warm-up 30 min., Z4 cool-down

Friday	Saturday	Sunday
Rest or easy ride	90-min. 'cross circuit 30-min. technique 60 min., Z4	3-hr. road ride, Z2

Friday	Saturday	Sunday
1-hr. ride, Z1	90-min. road ride, Z2	90-min. road ride, Z2

Friday	Saturday	Sunday
Rest or easy ride	2–3-hr. road ride, Z2	Race

Friday	Saturday	Sunday
Rest or easy ride	Race	Race

(continues)

TABLE 4.2 Sample Season Training Plan *(continued)*

Phase 4: December			
Monday	Tuesday	Wednesday	Thursday
A.M. 60–90-min. road ride, Z1	30-min. run (see text) 10-min. warm-up 10-min. hill repeats 10-min. cool-down	30-min. trainer 10-min. warm-up 20 min., Z4	25-min. run 10-min. warm-up 5 x 1-min., Z5
P.M.	1-hr. road ride, Z1	1-hr. skills session	1-hr. road ride, Z1 10 x 100 m sprints (see text)

Phase 5: January			
Monday	Tuesday	Wednesday	Thursday
A.M. 60–90-min. road ride, Z1	30-min. run (see text) 10-min. warm-up 10-min. hill repeats 10-min. cool-down	30-min. trainer 10-min. warm-up 20-min., Z4	25-min. run 3 x 3-min. intervals
P.M.	1-hr. road ride, Z3 10 x 150 m sprints (see text)		1-hr. road ride, Z2

Other Scheduling Considerations

Saturday races should be small, local competitions. But if Sunday's race is an important one, then Saturday's race should be replaced by a 1-hour Z1 road ride with four or five 15- to 20-second sprints.

Interval training is very hard, both mentally and physically. If at any time you have not recovered from a previous session (increased muscle soreness or an elevated resting heart rate in the morning will be the giveaway sign), replace the interval session with a recovery ride. If you start an interval session and after a good warm-up and a few intervals you are not seeing heart rates as high as you would expect, then cut the session short and rest up.

Friday	Saturday	Sunday
Rest or easy ride	Race or 3–4-hr. road ride, Z1, Z2	Race or 3–4-hr. road ride, Z1, Z2

Friday	Saturday	Sunday
Rest or easy ride	Race	Race

If you cannot discipline yourself to set intervals, replace them with "fartlek" training. Fartlek, or "speed play," is used by runners to give variety to their training. Sprint for signs, trees, lampposts, or to the top of a hill or down the other side. Without setting times or distances, fartlek still incorporates all the benefits of an interval session. Always allow time for a warm-up and a cool-down. Never start an interval session unless you have warmed up for at least 15 minutes (5–10 min. if running).

If you are forced to miss a day's training due to bad weather, illness, or weariness, do not be tempted to do more the next day to make up for it. Stick to your schedule. Complete your training diary, and note how you feel. You can refer back to the diary later to learn more about how different schedules or training levels affect your form.

Do not be tied down to these or any other schedules. If you feel you are not ready to move on to the next stage, carry on with the one you are in. Also, do not be afraid to taper your training prior to an important race.

Around Christmas and the New Year, depending on how the days fall, it is usually possible to race a number of times—and you should take advantage of this, as it is an excellent way to bring your form to a peak for the big races in January. Do not train hard between these races; just keep to recovery rides. Listen to what your body is telling you, and if you have not recovered fully, skip the next day's race.

If you are racing the U.S. National Championships, which are in early December, plan your season to peak on this weekend. If you are following the phases above, then simply start in August rather than September and take advantage of the longer evenings and better weather to add some volume to your Z1 and Z2 rides while you can.

On Fridays, you will notice that these schedules give you a choice between total rest and a steady ride. I favor total rest, but many people prefer a steady ride. If you cannot face the bike come Friday, keep off it; if you fancy a ride, go for it, but keep it steady.

REST AND RECOVERY

"My favorite training session? Sitting on the couch recovering!" Ryan Trebon, USA mountain-bike and cyclocross national champion told me. I would agree with him in one sense: The most important part of a good training regime is, in fact, resting.

The purpose of training is to place your body under physical stress over time so that it will adapt to the stresses imposed upon it and increase its ability to cope with greater stresses in the future. But your body needs time to adapt itself to the stress of training if it is to be of any benefit, and this comes in the form of rest.

Ryan Trebon is the American national champ in both 'cross and mountain bike in 2006 and the guy who defies the rule that a low center of gravity is an advantage for a 'cross rider!

Most athletes are motivated to train hard, but the riders who see rest as a sign of weakness are limiting the effects that their hard training can have on their body. You will perform better as a fresh rider who might be slightly undertrained than as a tired rider who is highly trained—although a fresh, highly trained rider would be optimum. Now that is not to say that for long periods of time you will be tired, as that is a by-product of training, but you simply must build cycles of recovery into your program to allow for development, whether it is a day a week in a short cycle, or a couple of weeks twice a year in a long cycle.

The need for rest is even greater if you work full-time, so you need to make sure recovery is a major part of your schedule. If you haven't been training long, taking two days off a week is a good idea. Mondays and Fridays are often good rest days, both physically and mentally: Physically, it is good to have consecutive days of hard work; mentally, taking Friday off helps you prepare for a good weekend of training or racing after a hard week; and resting again on Monday ensures you are recovered before you resume training on Tuesday.

A tired rider is never going to fill his or her potential, and there are times when compounded tiredness can cause significant health issues that require a long period of rest to recover from. The first stage of doing too much is better known as "overreaching." When this continues for a long period, or is accentuated by even more training or competition, it becomes "overtraining," which is more serious.

The symptoms for both conditions are similar, but they vary in terms of severity depending on how much damage has been done. The biggest difference is the recovery time required to return to healthy levels. The two main symptoms are fatigue and reduced performance, and the biggest problem for the athlete is how to recognize when these symptoms are the result of training too much. Seeing poor performance as a failure to train hard enough seems to be hardwired into an athlete's psyche, and the resulting effort to rectify the situation usually makes things worse.

Look for other symptoms as well, such as sleep disturbance, muscle soreness, a reduced maximum heart rate, and mood changes such as anxiety, depression, and stress and irritability. If you are experiencing some or all of these symptoms, or if you are constantly getting sniffles and picking up colds and viruses, then it's time to rest up.

But for how long? If the symptoms are transient, in that they're not present all the time but come and go, then you are more likely to be in the overreaching stage and your recovery can be counted in days and weeks. If the symptoms are persistent—present every day—then you may have caused some damage that could take weeks or months to repair. What you need to find is a sympathetic doctor who will respect your athletic lifestyle and treat you as a sportsperson and not an average man or woman in the street.

HOW TO PEAK FOR THE BIG DAY

Physically speaking, how to prepare for the race of the season has already been explained in the preceding sections—after a hard final training phase, the taper in the last week is achieved by decreasing the volume of training you are doing, but leaving in the intensity. This is a way of bringing you into form for a certain part of the season—in many cases, January and the national and World Championships.

The rest of peaking strategy is purely mental. You must concentrate on a certain number of races and these alone. All others are a means to an end—a step toward the next target race. The riders who treat every race identically, with the same amount of importance week in, week out, simply don't rise to the occasion when it matters. Obviously, the form has to be there, but when it is, the difference between you and the next person is in the mind.

Final preparations should be made during the week leading up to your big race. Resist the urge to fit in any last-minute panic training. If you haven't done it by now, it's too late; the best thing you can do is rest. Your training volume during this week should be low; cut out the time on the bike and replace it with quality rest to ensure that you are absolutely fresh for race day. But you do need to keep sparking your body with high-intensity efforts to keep it awake. During the last week, include a session of short, sharp intervals on both Tuesday and Thursday, but also reduce the number of these intervals by 40 to 50 percent from what you would do in a normal session. If you normally do ten intervals, then reduce that to six. Spend some time making sure your equipment is in top condition. You can put new tires on your bike (and your spare bike) early in the week, if needed, but any other new equipment should have been fitted a couple of weeks previously and used in training to ensure it is trouble-free.

For the rest of your final buildup, maintain your usual regime. Don't try any different foods, supplements, or sports drinks that might not agree with you; carry on eating sensibly, with an emphasis on, but not a major increase in, carbohydrates as you approach the weekend.

You may be nervous—and you should be nervous—but if you know your preparations have gone well, you can be confident that you will perform to your fullest potential.

Keeping a Training Diary

Once your season has been planned and your goals set, you and your coach should have a good idea of how to schedule your training. These plans—your training prescription—should be logged in a training diary, and then you should record the training you actually did, and pertinent details of how it went, as the training progresses throughout the season. And don't forget to highlight the big days when you have a goal.

As far as your coach is concerned, the more feedback you can give him or her, the better. A lot of coaching is reactive, so the training prescription may be amended and altered depending on how a previous session or block of sessions went. A good coach should be able to predict how you will cope with a certain workload, but if anything happens that could change the demands you put on your body, then your coach needs to know. This is especially the case if you have a long-distance coaching relationship whereby the coach might not have a detailed knowledge of the area you train in or be aware of the weather conditions you must cope with.

So, at the end of every day, you should note what training you have done, whether it departed from what you were supposed to do, how you felt, where you went, with whom, and what the weather was doing. A good addition to your diary could be a simple score for the session. Your coach should describe the session when he or she sets your training regime, and he or she should give it a score from one to five for how hard it should be. For example, a 2.5-hour Z2 ride with three 15-minute Z4 blocks might be rated a 3. If you complete the session perfectly as prescribed, but it was in very strong wind and it rained for the last hour, then that session might well have felt more like a 4 to you. If you can look at your records for a week and see discrepancies between the score set and the score feedback, then it's time to pick up the phone and have a chat about why they differ.

Keeping the feedback section of your training diary up-to-date will provide you and your coach with invaluable information, and the data that you record can cover a variety of bases. What should you record? That depends on the type of training session. If you performed a set of intervals, for example, record the times and the recoveries, the road you did the session on, the gearing you used, and any other useful information you can think of. For circuit and weight training, note the weights and the number of sets you completed. You may find it a real drag writing everything down in this way, and you might not see much point in it at the time. It is only afterward, when you are trying to find the form you had last year, that the true value of the training diary comes to light. Be honest with yourself when filling out your diary. If you felt terrible and went home after 20 minutes instead of finishing a 3-hour ride, then say so. If you don't, you are kidding nobody but yourself.

For race days, include details of the weather conditions, how you felt during the race, the results, and any comments you might have about your opponents—for instance, if any did not finish. As the season progresses, notice changes in their form that you can use to your advantage in forthcoming races. Also, log your equipment choices (tires or wheels, for example) as well as the tire pressures you used for that circuit. You will probably be back next year at the same race, and having a record of how the day went will enable you to make the right decisions about how to improve your performance next time around.

Record your resting heart rate daily, and your weight weekly. Note these at the same time of day and on the same day of the week each time. Also record the amount of sleep you had. Any variations to these figures can be symptoms of overreaching or overtraining, or possibly signs that you may be getting a cold or other illness. If you catch these signs early, you can take better care of yourself, get plenty of rest, and possibly ward off the illness or limit its duration.

Full-Time Training

What makes someone a world champion?

Over the years, in all the talks I've had with leading 'cross riders, two things have struck home: First, it's surprising how many of them do very similar training; their sessions may not be exactly the same, but the volume of training and the pattern of their weeks during the season are very similar. Second, they all train incredibly hard, and it always takes a few years to be able to tolerate that kind of a workload. But if what they do in training is so similar, what is it that makes the difference between a world champion and someone who crosses the finish line in the teens in the same races? For the great champions, it doesn't come down to training volume or quality; it's how they live life and deal with the other "stuff" around the training that makes the difference.

And I guess that makes sense; after all, there is only so much training the human body can cope with, and if all the champs are doing very similar styles and amounts of it, then it comes down not just to physiology and the genes you were gifted with, but other, less tangible factors. We know that if you go down the world ranking, certainly for the men, you usually have to go pretty deep, and certainly past the top twenty, before you find anyone who is trying to fit a job in around his or her life as a bike rider. So it's not time to train or recover that is the answer. For the women, the situation is slightly different due to the lack of financial rewards available in cycling and the necessity to supplement their incomes; even current world champ Maryline Salvetat works pretty much full-time in the medical profession.

We know that the training week from September to February is very similar for all of the guys: Monday rest or short recovery ride, Tuesday long endurance ride for up to 4 hours, Wednesday morning shorter endurance ride of a couple of hours followed by group 'cross training, Thursday motorpacing for between 1 and 2 hours, Friday recovery ride, then Saturday and Sunday races.

We know that a lot of them try to find some warm sun to train in where they can do a bigger endurance block, usually four or five weeks before the European National Championships and seven or eight weeks before the Worlds. Sure, some run a few times a week and some avoid it altogether, some train alone and some in groups; but aside from these minor variations it's all very similar. None of that seems to make the difference between a Sven Nys and a Robert Glazja.

So, maybe it's the work carried out during the summer that makes the difference. That makes more sense than looking too hard at the training during the winter. It's common knowledge that you make the biggest jumps between seasons, when you can focus on training hard without the distraction of important competition. And unlike the road, where riders specialize and peak for certain events during the summer over a period of a few weeks, the spring classics, one of the tours, or the Worlds, unless a 'cross rider is injured or sick, he or she pretty much races a full season, with something scheduled every weekend.

So the summer can make a difference, and it's worth paying it some serious attention. But the rest of the story is told by just how much of your life you are willing to sacrifice in pursuit of excellence.

That, along with the all-important genes, over which you have no control, seems to make the biggest difference.

Exactly how much sacrifice and dedication are we talking here? Well, it's significant: Life revolves around bike riding and racing, and not the other way around. Holidays, when they happen, have to fit into year plans; celebrations for weddings, birthdays, and Christmas, Hanukkah, or Kwanzaa all happen without you, unless they fall during the few days a year when you can afford to stay up late and party. Relationships take longer to develop, as there is so little time available to do the "normal" things that see relationships blossom. Diet revolves around functional nutrition as a fuel and a recovery aid, with taste and variety an added bonus. And when it gets really serious the bedroom is converted into a sealed unit with a humming machine in the corner controlling the environment so you can replicate altitude training and grow more red blood cells as you sleep!

Life is a constant vision of a rainbow jersey. If you are competing for the top slot, you know that if Sven is ultimate and you need to beat him, then you must either be equally as ultimate and hope he has bad luck or you must wait until he retires. Not much of a choice there!

If you decide that this is the life for you, think about whether you are willing to make these sacrifices to pursue your dream. You need to examine what training full-time entails. If your situation means that training full-time is not possible for you, but you still want to make the most of the time you have, you should seek your coach's advice, decide what is best for your individual circumstances, and then work out a schedule. If you can train full-time, use the suggestions below to begin to develop a plan that will work best for you.

Remember that training must be progressive. If you are presently training for only ten hours a week, don't try to double it to twenty hours straightaway. Your body will not be able to cope with it, and you will wear yourself out quickly. Gradually build up the hours, and when you can cope with the time involved, then—and only then—

start to increase the intensity of the efforts. No intense or interval training should be attempted until a solid background of conditioning work has been achieved.

If you are considering altering your circumstances to give yourself an opportunity to train and race full- or near full-time, then try to begin in the summertime and not simply on October 1 in time for the season. You will make bigger gains in fitness and ability during your off-season (the summer) than you would by going straight into an intensive winter. Starting off with an intensive winter, you would make gains, but these would be more from increased recovery time after races and hard training than from increased training itself. You will make better gains in fitness and conditioning if you get a good solid summertime full of riding. The summertime approach will be more likely to give you the increase in performance that you gave up your job for.

CHAPTER 5

Training Components

Indoor Trainers

The indoor trainer has become an almost essential piece of equipment for any serious bike rider, especially those who want to train or compete during the winter.

Although there is an ever-increasing number of indoor trainers on the market, based on different technologies and designs, the basic principle is the same: to create a resistance on the rear wheel while pedaling. Your budget and the space you have available for an indoor trainer will be primary considerations when deciding on a purchase, but in the end it may just come down to personal preference. There are a number of portable and fold-up designs on the market, and these can be especially useful because you can take them with you when you travel—especially to races for use during the pre-race warm-up. Some models consist of rollers, with no resistance, which you must balance on as you ride a complete bike. These are excellent for developing leg speed and an efficient pedaling style, and also for balance. Riders who have trouble riding rollers well definitely need to develop their core stability.

Trainers that incorporate a magnetic or fluid resistance unit are much quieter than the old first-generation fan models and usually have fixed increments of resistance. As a general rule, if you are going to use the trainer regularly in one place, if you have enough space for it, and if you do not need to travel with it, a rigid system—where you remove the front wheel and place the forks into the frame—is a good idea. If space is limited and you wish to take the trainer to events, then the fold-up, A-frame units are best. And as they are significantly quieter than they used to be, you can use one for warming up in the hotel lobby or even training in your room, provided, of course, you don't do maximum-effort sessions late into the night and disturb the other guests.

ADVANTAGES OF INDOOR TRAINERS

Possibly the greatest advantage of working out on an indoor trainer is that it is so safe for interval training, as you need not look where you're going or watch for traffic. You can also control your heart rate zone more efficiently for longer periods of work, as there are no breaks in your momentum like those you would experience on the open road. On the road, you must contend with hills, headwinds, stoplights, traffic, and so on. Not so on the indoor trainer. Nor do you have to quit when the sun goes down or miss your session because of snow or rain. With an indoor trainer, you have complete control over your training, with no influence from external factors.

DISADVANTAGES OF INDOOR TRAINERS

Compared to the advantages, the disadvantages of working out on an indoor trainer are few. But long sessions can be mind-numbingly dull without something to watch or listen to. A DVD of your favorite race can be inspiring, and of course indoor training is what iPods were invented for! The better indoor trainers are programmable so that you can duplicate racecourse slopes or interactive so that you can have some competition; many models display a full range of information, such as power output, heart rate, RPM, and speed, to keep your interest up.

Another drawback is that it can get uncomfortable working out indoors. If you do not have a fan or are in a badly ventilated area, training this way can become difficult. Make sure you invest in a good fan, and always have a water bottle close by.

The only other potential, if unlikely, disadvantage is that you may start to rely on the trainer too much. If you begin to get lazy, you may not want to go outside in the cold to ride. Although indoor training has its place for controlling safe, high-intensity workouts, remember that it is only a substitute—you must also keep training in an environment that approximates racing conditions, and that doesn't mean doing a session on your trainer outside in the rain!

INDOOR TRAINING HINTS

You can make your indoor training sessions much more comfortable by following a few simple guidelines. For example, don't overdress for a training session. Shorts and an undervest will be enough, with possibly an extra jersey to start with if you are in an unheated garage.

The area where you train should be well ventilated and not too warm. You may find that opening a door or window provides enough fresh air. A temperature above 68 degrees Fahrenheit (20 degrees Celsius) is too hot, so keep away from any sources of heat, such as radiators. You may need a large cooling fan if you are going to train indoors. Overheating can have serious consequences, affecting training levels and target heart rates. You should also have a drinking bottle handy while training, and always make sure you are well hydrated before you start a session.

Finally, if you train in a garage or outbuilding, make sure the floor is free of dust—if there is dust the trainer's fan will blow it around and you'll end up inhaling it, and this is not a good idea.

INDOOR TRAINER WORKOUTS

Although the cyclocross rider will use the indoor trainer mainly for high-intensity workouts, it also can be employed for endurance work as well as warm-ups for races. Follow the tips below for each type of workout.

Endurance Work

If the weather forces you to stay indoors for an endurance session, the indoor trainer is a great alternative. Warm up for 5 to 10 minutes, then ride for an hour at the Z3 level and end with a 5-minute cool-down. If you find it difficult to sustain the Z3 level for that long, break it down into four 15-minute blocks with 5-minute recoveries between blocks, then progress to three blocks of 20 minutes and two blocks of 30 minutes. At that point, you will be ready to tackle an hour.

Strength and Power Sessions

Strength and power workouts are of a higher training intensity and shorter duration than endurance workouts and are aimed at improving your ability to maintain a speed just above race pace for short periods. In a cyclocross race, you'll need to draw on this skill during the starting effort and when you are attacking other riders.

Play around with medium-length intervals (of 2–5 minutes) where you are riding at a threshold effort that you could maintain for, say, a 10-minute time trial (typically at the top of Z4), but incorporate short efforts at the Z5 level before going back down to Z4.

For example, you could warm up for 5 to 10 minutes, then ride for 3 minutes mostly at Z4, but with the last 20 seconds of each minute at Z5. One block requires four efforts with 2 minutes of recovery riding between them. Or, you could warm up for 5 to 10 minutes, then ride for 2 minutes at Z4, 1 minute at Z5, and 2 more at Z4, for a total of 5 minutes. For a block, do three of these 5-minute efforts with 3 minutes of recovery riding between them.

Another alternative is a "pyramid" session, in which you increase the duration of the work interval up to a point, then decrease it toward the end of the session. This type of workout is particularly good for developing your strength and mimics the efforts often found in races. Start with a 1-minute work interval at Z4/Z5 with 1 minute of recovery. Then increase each subsequent work interval by 30 seconds until you reach a 3-minute work interval. At that point, reduce each successive interval by 30 seconds until you are back at 1 minute, and the session is completed. You will have completed 17 minutes of intervals plus 8 minutes of recoveries for a total time of 25 minutes. When this becomes easy, add another interval at the top. For a shorter but tough session, begin with a 15-second work interval followed by a 15-second recovery; then go to 30 seconds with a 30-second recovery, 45 seconds with a 45-second recovery, and 60 seconds with a 60-second recovery; and finally back down to 45 seconds, 30 seconds, and 15 seconds, with the same recoveries as above. Start with two pyramids with a 5-minute recovery spin between them, and increase by half a pyramid as you become stronger until you reach a maximum of four.

Speed Endurance

As the season progresses, you will want to improve your speed endurance—that is, your ability to make repeated fast efforts over short distances of around 400 meters.

Training for this typically involves making repeated efforts with short recovery times between efforts. As you adapt to these sessions, aim to reduce the recovery time and increase the number of work intervals. These sessions should last only about 20 minutes, but they are performed at maximum effort. Heart rate is not an ideal indicator for these workouts but will be in the Z5/Z6 range.

After the normal warm-up, do ten 1-minute intervals with 1 minute of recovery between them. As you adapt to the stress, reduce the recovery time by 10 seconds, but leave the effort length the same.

Tapering before Championships

When your training reaches a peak just before the end-of-season championship races, you need to taper your training as part of race preparation. This means very short intervals at maximum intensity with relatively little recovery.

As you approach the tapering-down period in the couple of weeks before the big race, try reducing the interval time to 30 seconds with a 30-second recovery, but also reduce the number in a set, so you might only do six of these.

Cyclocross Training

Actual on-the-dirt cyclocross training should start as soon as your summer race season starts to wind down. If you compete on the mountain-bike circuit, then you've just had a summer of riding off-road, so there's no real hurry. You'll need a gentle reminder of the things that you cannot do on a 'cross bike that you can do on a mountain bike, but a couple of falls or punctures will soon refresh your memory. If you ride exclusively on the road all summer, you'll need to start a little earlier—say, in early September. Reacquaint yourself with the techniques required and sharpen up your skills before starting any serious training on your 'cross bike.

If you live in an area where the varied terrain used in cyclocross is available, take single-loop 3- to 4-hour rides on your 'cross bike. Riding with a small group is a tremendous way of getting into shape while working on specific skills, and group rides are great fun. If you are stuck in an area where this is not possible, replace group training with long road rides, preferably on roads as hilly as possible. You should try to fit these rides in twice a week during September.

In October, your 'cross training should take place on a smaller circuit, but not so small that you get bored training on it for an hour. A circuit that takes 6 to 10 minutes to complete is ideal. Your 'cross sessions should incorporate some higher zone work, especially if there are a few of you and it gets competitive, and if this is done on the same circuit, then you can gauge your progress during the season. Again, try to get involved in group training on the circuit. If a group doesn't already exist in your area, then simply find somewhere accessible, legal, and fun to ride and get started.

Training with a group on a regular basis can provide a boost. As German cyclocross champion Mike Kluge, a big fan of group training, said, "Cyclocross is hard enough; if it's possible always try to find a group to train with. It's more fun, you can practice better, and it brings competitiveness. Of course, people live in different places, but you just have to arrange it. If you train alone and you have a bad day, then you won't get better, but if one of the group has good motivation, and that motivation dumps on you, then suddenly you can turn your day around."

Examples of quality training groups are numerous, and some are legendary, from Kluge's Berlin session in the Groenewald in Germany to Mario De Clerq's group training in the woods at the top of the Kluisberg in Belgium. In England, there's a weekly group training session on a single 2-hour loop in Derbyshire, and in Holland day-long sessions are held by Coach Nico Van Hest in Alphen near Tilburg. The national team trains for 2 hours every Wednesday morning, followed by general training for anyone from kids to veterans to novice women in the afternoon. Once word gets around that a group is out there, people will travel to join it; it's the 'cross equivalent of "If you build it, they will come"!

Once the season begins, your 'cross training does not need to last for much more than an hour. With 10 to 15 minutes each for warm-up and cool-down, this leaves 40 to 50 minutes for the hard efforts, which should be varied from session to session to keep boredom from creeping in. Vary the circuits on certain days, or reverse the direction, and stick to these circuits all season. The Dutch group mentioned above changes sessions depending on the style of race that weekend. You can add run-ups, sand, mud, hurdles, and climbs to the session depending on the focus of the next race. This strategy makes the practices specific for a purpose but keeps them varied and interesting as well.

While training, you should always try to time your efforts, laps, and recoveries. Having a coach do this is ideal, but you can also use the stopwatch on your heart rate monitor or insert markers in your heart rate files as you start each lap.

The lengths of intervals and recoveries should always be recorded in your training diary for future reference. This will make it easier to measure your progress over time and help you determine when to intensify your efforts.

Road Training

Road training is a year-round occupation and the mainstay of your training routine, whether you race 'cross, road, track, or mountain bike. Nevertheless, you should vary it according to the time of year, the races you are preparing for, and the stage of your training "cycle."

No two weeks will be exactly the same in road training unless you are spending some time building an endurance base of long, steady distance miles. And even endurance should be built up steadily, preferably over a three- to- five-week cycle followed by an easier "recovery" week.

After a break from the summer season of road racing or mountain biking, you should resume training, building endurance through the end of September. Focus on quality endurance rides, and remember, you are still building condition, so while the weather is still good take advantage of it and put in as many hours as you can with some rides up to the 3- or 4-hour mark. By the time you get into the swing of the season and start racing in mid-October, most of your sessions on the road will be closer to 2 or 2.5 hours. As the season progresses, you will slightly reduce the total time you spend on the road, although, as mentioned earlier, many riders still like to have one long day per week when they ride for 3 to 4 hours.

Once you get into the holiday season, avoid the temptation to train with the road racers, who at this point have just awakened from their winter slumbers and are beginning to get the miles in. It might be fun and sociable, but it will not do much to help you meet your end-of-season goals in January. Instead, you might want to try "motorpacing." The Belgian racers use motorpacing weekly, and it is a very effective way to train. If it's accessible to you, or you can find a friend with a small motorcycle who agrees to try it with you, then as an aid to attaining increased speed and condition it is unbeatable. A motorcycle can be used in two main ways: to produce steady-state riding at a high cadence and intensity or as an interval session where the motorcycle is used as a "rabbit" to chase. This is a great way to stay focused—you try to stay with the pacer as he/she gradually increases the speed on the flat, or you try to keep up as the pacer maintains a steady speed up gradual climbs.

But a word of warning regarding motorpacing: While in Belgium and other European countries there is no problem training in this way and you will not draw any interest from the local law-enforcement agencies, in other countries, and certainly in the United States, it is an illegal practice in many jurisdictions. You must be aware of the laws where you live or where you intend to train.

Also be aware of the increased dangers of training behind a motorcycle and avoid training behind a car; visibility is poor, and you become a far greater traffic hazard behind a car than behind a small motorcycle. Make sure you and the driver of the motorcycle have a clear set of rules and signals to use for things such as sudden stops, potholes, intersections, and other traffic.

Weight Training

Weight training can be a useful and enjoyable part of your workout schedule, and it's the best way to isolate and strengthen certain muscles that fatigue quickly. These muscles are important in cycling, but they are not worked in isolation when you are cycling and will not strengthen significantly as a result of cycling alone. The best examples are your forearms, upper arms, shoulders, and back, all of which at times can ache as much as your legs during and after a hard race.

Decide for yourself how much weight training you need. For instance, if you have a manual-labor job where you use upper body strength daily, you may not need to use weight training to strengthen your arms and shoulders. But if you sit at a desk all day, then you probably could use some extra work.

If you are intimidated by the thought of working out in a gym or you don't know where to begin with free weights, relax. It's not necessary to use free weights, which in the hands of a beginner can be awkward and even unsafe. Equipment at the gym has come so far technologically that virtually any muscle can be worked on a machine without the risk of injury.

To design your weight-training program, enlist the aid of an experienced person, such as an instructor or personal trainer at a good gym. If you explain what it is you are trying to achieve, the instructor or trainer should be able to help you plan a program that includes all the appropriate muscles. To increase the muscular endurance of each one, perform a high number of repetitions at a relatively low weight. Muscular power, developed by using heavy weights with few repetitions, is not what you are aiming for. You are not looking to become a bodybuilder on a bike, and you don't want to drag extra weight uphill.

If you decide to take on a weight program, then you will need to be consistent. At first, try to fit in a session of weights at least twice a week—three times, if possible, for the best effect—and continue the program throughout both the off-season and the race season. If after a race you notice that one body part is aching more than the others, concentrate on building up your strength in the muscles that are affected.

Weight training has to be progressive to work. Don't perform the same exercises week in and week out at the same weight and same number of repetitions. Start at a comfortable weight at which you can perform three sets of 15 repetitions. Then do two sets of 15 reps and one of 20, then one of 15 and two of 20, then three of 20. When you can do that, increase the weight and drop back to three sets of 15 reps.

If you cannot manage 15 reps of an exercise, the weight is too heavy, so reduce it. Don't worry: Your strength will increase quite quickly in the early stages—you won't be using the bar without any weights on it for long!

Always start your weight-training session with a stretching routine to warm up, followed by 5 minutes on an exercise bike or running machine. After the weight-training session, pedal gently on the stationary bike to cool down and stretch any muscles that feel tight. Use the following exercises as the basis for your program. Add others based on the machines available at your gym and your instructor's advice.

1. Hip abductor
2. Hip adductor
3. Leg extensions, single
4. Leg curls, single or double
5. Calf raises
6. Bench press, lying or seated
7. Pull-downs, standing or sitting

8. Lateral raises
9. Triceps push-down
10. Upright rowing

In addition to the above, you can supplement your program with the following:

11. Sit-ups
12. Back hyperextensions
13. Chin-ups
14. Hanging leg raises, which do not require the use of weights

Circuit Training

As an all-round fitness training regime, circuit training is highly recommended. If time allows, it can be carried out both pre-season and in-season.

Circuit training comprises a number of exercises in a gym—some using apparatus, others not—that work different groups of muscles and the cardiovascular system. Each exercise is performed in turn, usually for 1 minute, during which time you attempt to do as many repetitions of the exercise as possible. After a very brief, timed rest (either the same as your effort time while a partner performs the exercises or simply as long as it takes you to get to the next "station"), you move on to the next one, and so on, usually for ten to twelve exercises. The complete circuit is then repeated a second or third time, depending on the fitness of the participants.

Make no mistake: Circuit training done properly is exhausting. If it isn't, either you are not trying hard enough or the recovery time is too long. After an initial session of stretching and jogging to warm up, followed by the circuits and a cool-down, you will have probably spent an hour working—but the effects will feel like much more. Circuit training is a great way to get in a high-zone session if the weather is bad, and if the majority of your other riding is more steady-state, such as in commuting miles, it can serve simply as a once-a-week blast.

Circuits are best done in pairs, with one participant resting while the other works. This method also introduces a competitive element into the training, as scores can be compared. A number of cycling clubs offer circuit-training classes, particularly during the winter, but if you cannot find a club that does this, try a local sports or fitness center. If you still draw a blank, consider making a home circuit using the exercises that do not require apparatus. But you must be strict with the timing of the effort and recovery periods, as it is too easy to cheat when unsupervised.

If you want to do circuit training at home, try the exercises listed below. Spend 40 seconds per exercise, and after finishing one, go straight to the next. Use whatever you have available to achieve the moves. For example, you can use a solid, low chair against a wall for step-ups, a couple of chairs together for the raises and extensions, and paint cans for bicep curls. Be imaginative, but remember, safety is paramount. Make sure any makeshift equipment is up to the task, you are using correct form, and at the very least the lids are firmly in place on your paint cans!

1. Push-ups
2. Sit-ups
3. Standing squats
4. Squat thrusts
5. Lunges
6. Jumping jacks
7. Jump Rope
8. Hip raises
9. Back extensions
10. Bicep curls

Core Strength Training

In recent years, core strength training (or core stability training), which develops the muscles of the stomach, back, and hips, has become one of the hottest areas in the fitness field, and increasing numbers of bike riders have come to realize that core training gives you more than a nice six-pack: It also improves performance and reduces injuries.

The main muscles to develop in core training are the transversus abdominis, the deep muscles of the stomach that circle your mid-section like a corset; the lower abdominals, the muscles in your lower back that surround and support your spine; and the internal obliques, which are deep inside the stomach, to the side. All these are very important for correct posture, but for 'cross riders they are also crucial to developing a strong platform for the action of the leg muscles. In other words, core strength helps your leg muscles do their work of propelling your bike forward, while stabilizing your body by giving you better balance.

Core strength is something you can see in a rider if you know what to look for. The next time you are watching a race, look at the riders at the front of the pack and compare their riding style to the riders who are lagging behind. If you can, watch a video of the top riders with this in mind. The ones in front will look relaxed but "solid" on their bikes. Their legs turn the pedals, but without any additional, unnecessary movement from the torso and upper body, and their bodies are constantly adapting in position to deal with the balance required on any particular section. When one of the leaders laps a tail-ender, the difference in style becomes even more apparent. The slower riders will likely move some parts of their body in time with their legs, and when they try to balance they may have to stop pedaling. That is a crucial loss. Even a couple of revs lost in a corner or in deep sand or mud trying to stay balanced reduce speed, and the seconds lost cannot be regained. Besides losing the time that was spent focusing on balancing instead of pedaling, the rider loses momentum and has to work harder to get back up to speed.

So that's why it's necessary to have a strong core, but how do you improve it? There are two possibilities: You can enroll in a Pilates class or you can work out in a home session. The advantage of starting with a Pilates class is that you will learn the correct technique, which you can then take away with you to continue in your home sessions. In addition, in a class you will be encouraged to move on to more progressive exercises as your strength increases. If you have never done Pilates before and you start at home, then you can pick up some information from illustrated books or DVDs. If you go this route, then check out the "Recommended Reading" section of this book for the best advice on the subject. Of course, you can also do a Web search to find out more about Pilates.

As a starting point, try the following. Do these exercises in the order shown, spending 60 seconds on each. Rest for 15 seconds before moving on to the next exercise. After completing all six, take a 5-minute break and repeat the entire series. Try to do this routine three times a week.

1. **Step-Downs**

   Lie on your back with one hand under your lower back. Lift your legs so that your thighs are at a 90-degree angle to the floor, and bend both knees to a 90-degree angle. Slowly lower your right foot to within 1 inch of the floor while tightening your lower back so that it does not move up and down during the maneuver. Keep your right leg bent at a 90-degree angle and maintain the position of your left leg. Hold your right foot 1 inch off the floor for 5 seconds, then return it to the starting position next to the left leg. Repeat the same action, but this time with the left foot.

   Repeat both sequences three to five times.

2. **Prone Stabilizer**

   Start on your stomach, then raise yourself into a modified push-up position with all your weight balanced on your forearms and toes. Keep your back as straight as possible. Then, slowly raise your left leg until it lines up with your back. Hold this position for 5 seconds, then lower your left leg. Repeat with right leg.
   Repeat both sequences three to five times.

3. **Bridge**

   Lie on your back with your arms beyond your head and with your feet planted on the floor directly below your knees. Press down on your feet and lift your torso and upper legs until they form a straight line. With your weight on your shoulders and feet, slowly extend the right leg by straightening the knee. Be sure to keep your back straight. Hold for 5 seconds, then repeat with the left leg.
   Repeat both sequences three to five times.

4. **Side Stabilizer**

   Lie on your right side with your right elbow under your shoulder and your left foot resting on your right foot. Press down with your forearm and foot until you lift your body off the ground. Keep your body as straight as possible, not allowing your hips to sag. Hold this position in a controlled fashion for 30 seconds. Repeat on your left side.
   Repeat both sequences three to five times.

5. **Fire Hydrant**

   Start on your hands and knees. Maintaining the 90-degree angle of your left knee, lift your left leg until the thigh is parallel to your upper body. Hold for 5 seconds, then lower. Repeat the same motion, but this time continue it by forcing the knee as far to the left as possible. Hold for 5 seconds. Repeat these steps, but this time force the knee and thigh as far as possible to the right, crossing over your body's midline. Hold for 5 seconds.
   Repeat both sequences three to five times.

6. Supine Stabilizer

Lie on your back with your legs fully extended. With your elbows under your shoulders, lift your entire body onto your forearms and heels. Keep your legs, hips, and back as straight as possible. While maintaining this position, lift your left leg 4 inches off the floor and hold for 5 seconds. Repeat with your right leg.

Repeat both sequences three to five times.

Remember, a lot of core exercises are about very slight movements and control of the muscles, so technique is everything. Slow, total control is the key.

Stretching

One aspect of your training routine that should never be missed is a daily dose of stretching. You can recognize the cyclists who don't stretch; they hobble around as if they're suffering from premature aging.

Cycling keeps your muscles in a contracted state, meaning that your arms, legs, and back do not operate through their full range of movement while riding. It is important that this be remedied off the bike through a comprehensive routine of stretches to avoid injury and lessen the risk of muscular strains and soreness. A good stretch can have the same effect as a massage, removing waste from the muscles and helping recovery.

You should stretch before and after every training session as well as first thing in the morning (especially if you run then). You should also stretch out before bed if you feel stiff after a hard day's training. Stretching doesn't take long—only a matter of minutes per session—and you can fit it in while watching television at the end of a hard day and/or as part of your core-strength routines.

HINTS FOR EFFECTIVE STRETCHING

- Do not stretch too far. Find a slight stretch, and hold it at that point for around 30 seconds. The point of stretch should never be painful.
- Never bounce. Bouncing tightens the very muscles you are trying to stretch, so stretch gently and hold it.
- Breathe slowly and deeply. Concentrate on the muscle you are stretching, and relax.
- Never rush a set of stretches.
- Do not try to match yesterday's efforts. You will be naturally stiffer or looser on some days than on others.
- Do not compare yourself with others—everybody is different and has different levels of flexibility.
- Regular stretching is the key. Little and often is better than a lot every now and then.

People tend to spend more time on the first leg, arm, or area they stretch, and they usually stretch their "easy" or more flexible side first. To even out the differences in flexibility in your body, stretch your tight side first.

Remember those riders who were hobbling around? Take a look at them on their bikes, and you will probably notice that they don't look quite right. They usually appear to be sitting too low and too far forward, riding on the front of the saddle. A lack of mobility means that they cannot pedal in the most efficient position on the bike, so they set the bike up in a fashion that feels comfortable but that actually adds to their problems. Still, you stretch, your position is right, and you beat them anyway, so what do you care?

Training for Women

From a physical perspective, I recommend the same training principles and sessions for women as I do for men. But there are some aspects of training that should take priority for women. Often, the biggest gains for women come not from increasing fitness or strength, but from practicing and perfecting the technical aspects of 'cross.

Ideally, gains in fitness and technical ability should grow at a similar rate: As you get fitter and faster on your bike, your ability to go around corners, dismount, shoulder your bike, jump hurdles, and so on should improve accordingly. But the reality is that for women gains in fitness come faster than gains in technique. You may find that you can go fast into a corner but can't get around it, or that you have the strength to ride a muddy climb but not the confidence. It's worth spending proportionately more time honing technical skills; when skills are perfect, then fitness can play catch-up if necessary.

At the top level in the men's game, the differences among the front-runners in fitness and technique are pretty small, but fitness comes out on top every time. For the women in the front, it's often a different story. A supremely fit woman can still miss the podium if she is not up to speed on the other aspects of her race, and if a woman can have the technical side of her game down (especially at a younger age), then as gains in fitness and strength come more naturally in later years, that rider will succeed over the ones who never quite got around to working on their cornering technique or hurdling style.

If you are a woman 'cross rider, try training with other women to keep your motivation strong. You may find that the spirit of competition and camaraderie is stronger with a female riding partner or group. Concentrate on perfecting aspects of the sport where good technique can make up for less upper body strength. For example, learn how to pick up the bike quickly (remember, a moving bike picked up

One of the most talented female cyclists in the sport,
Marianne Vos from Holland won Elite World Championships
and World Cups in both road racing and cyclocross
before the age of 20.

quickly is "lighter" than a bike picked up slowly from a standstill),
how to ride efficiently in deep mud or sand, and how to run on steep
runs or stairs. Devote time to learning how to corner and how to
"read" lines, courses, and surfaces, as they can change rapidly during
races. Practice any areas of the circuit that require your best friend,
momentum, until you can perform them smoothly and effectively.

And finally, if you have male friends who try to take charge at
races, or even during your training—telling you where to ride, what
gear to be in, and so on—explain that you need to make these decisions yourself. You are the athlete, and you'll learn faster when you

---

STARTING OUT

Early in my cyclocross career, I know I made people laugh a lot. I would get to hurdles and basically stop, get off the bike, go across, get back on, and keep going. My first few races were local, small races. Because I had a good gap I was able to go over the hurdles without technique. Stu Thorne would come to 'cross practice and show me how to get on and off. Getting off was not that hard . . . it was getting back on. I would ride around before the race and really focus on trying to get on and off bike. It took me a few years before I finally omitted the double step (that was funny, too)—but I've got it dialed in by now.

LYNE BESSETTE

---

carry out the responsibilities that go with that role. Pre-ride a course by yourself and make your own judgments about it. Even if you make mistakes, you'll learn from them like any other athlete. Put together your own bike, pump up the tires, and make your own decisions about which wheels and tires to run, when to start your warm-up, and how many layers of clothing you need to warm up in. If you want advice, go ahead and ask for it, but remember that you are the one who is racing, and you are the one in charge. When you choose a coach, make sure your choice is someone who will give you the same respect that he or she gives to male clients.

Running

Running plays at least a small part in most 'cross races. At some point in nearly every race, you're going to be on your feet, and every once in a while, when it's wet and muddy, you will need to run a lot. Ergo, it makes sense to consider incorporating some running into your training. With the recent trend in race circuits toward faster races with fewer runs, the importance of heavy running sessions has declined somewhat. Nevertheless, if you start running regularly, one wet winter you might be glad you did. Moreover, as a form of cross-training (as an alternative to cycling), running is ideal. It will make you a fitter, better conditioned, better overall athlete whether you actually have to run a lot in your races or not. Some riders feel the benefits of regular running even when on the bike, and as a high-quality session, it cannot be faulted. Even if your running only takes place in the pre-season buildup, then fades away as more on-the-bike training takes over, it will still have been worth it.

Running is a superb way in itself to improve the cardiovascular system. But the most important goal of your running program should be to boost your ability to run well during a race. The runs you need to be able to perform in a race are likely to be short and sharp—either up a hill or steps or over a piece of ground that is too muddy to ride. To reflect this, your running training should incorporate short and sharp efforts—bank runs and stairs, for example. But, of course, this type of focused training will only be productive if you have that base of running miles. In this way, it is similar to cycling.

All of your running should be on grass, if possible, on a running track, or at least on a smooth surface. The jarring effect of running on roads makes the supple muscles of a cyclist very sore, and injuries can develop easily. If you are running cross-country, make sure that your footwear is up to the conditions.

If bad weather during the winter keeps you off your bike, then substitute a session of running. In a 20- to 30-minute run, you can do as much work as in a much longer bike ride. Bad weather is not such a problem with running, as you are generating a lot of heat; running keeps your hands and feet moving, and there is not as much windchill as with cycling because you are moving at slower speeds. And, of course, you are out for a relatively short time.

Running should not be attempted without a good jog and stretch to warm up, especially if done first thing in the morning. If possible, start your running program at the beginning of the season, in August, with three sessions a week. Begin with a leisurely 10- to 15-minute run, then build up to 30 minutes at a steady pace by the end of September. In October, you should start on a schedule that will take you through the season. Try to run for 20 to 25 minutes two or three mornings a week. You should be covering considerably more distance by this time than you were in August. This schedule should stay about the same as the season progresses; only the intensity will increase as you become faster.

Pure interval work during these runs is not really necessary, as you will be getting enough higher-zone training on your indoor trainer as well as 'cross sessions to simulate the efforts of a race. Doing large amounts of high-zone work is not a good idea: It overworks you physically and is also hard mentally. So keep your daily runs enjoyable but still fairly fast.

If you are of the opinion that keeping running as part of your training may cost you speed on the bike, then give it a miss after the beginning of October when you start racing. Simply do the initial preseason runs to help get you in shape, then focus on cycling. If you do this, make sure you get adequate practice running with your bike during 'cross sessions. If you end up farther back in races than you know you are capable of, or notice that you're getting dropped on the running sections, then look seriously at making running a more permanent part of your schedule.

Training for Under-16 Racers

Juvenile racing is the place where most of the stars of today made their first appearance, whether in a circuit race on the road, a 'cross race, a local time trial, or a small mountain-bike race.

Just imagine: Some of these kids could race for ten years and still only be 15! In Britain every race promotion has to include a race for the under-12s; the only requirements are a bike and a helmet.

Juvenile or junior racing is the ideal place to learn racing. But it is important not to specialize in one branch of cycling at an early age; you should try everything going. Even if as a senior rider you end up deciding that 'cross or mountain-bike racing is for you, to compete at a high level you must at least be proficient on the road to benefit from the fitness it will give you. Success cannot be gained in a six-month season—ride as many juvenile races on the road, track, and mountain bike as you can. The experience will pay off later.

What's most important is just to enjoy riding your bike. Training seriously and the complicated business of working out training schedules, getting enough interval training in, lifting weights, and so on should be left until you are a junior at least, or preferably a senior. By then you will have finished growing, gotten the business of studying and taking exams out of the way, and reached a point where you can decide what sort of effort and commitment you want to put into your racing.

At the same time, you should not limit your sporting involvement to cycling. Involve yourself in as many sports as you can while the facilities are available to you at school. All of them will help you with your cycling. A cyclocross rider needs to be able to do more than just ride a bike fast. He or she must be strong, agile, and flexible; have a solid core; and be able to run, jump, and carry a bike—and all of this takes more than just pure cycling to achieve. Participating in a variety of sports can improve your athleticism.

If you are keen on 'cross and looking for success at an early age, you should plan your program with great care—if possible, under the guidance of a coach. Do not be quick to compare yourself with other riders your own age, or your training with their training. Some people mature faster than others, and their success may simply be a result of their increased strength; others who grow more slowly might find themselves slipping back in performance in relation to their friends or teammates, but they will catch up later. Results are hard to compare at this age, but solid, well-rounded training will eventually pay off. And don't copy some training schedule from an elite rider you find in a magazine!

It is probably easier for a late developer to continue with a cycling career than for someone who matured early and found success easily with little effort to stay on top. By the time they've reached 18 or 20, most people have grown to their full extent, and those who have had early success will have to increase their efforts significantly to stay ahead—often, training becomes too much effort and they are lost to the sport.

The record books are full of juvenile and junior medal-winners who have faded away because the going got tough. But if you look farther down the same result tables, you will find a lot of names of people who are now top riders who found their success later on through hard work. A good example is the skinny 17-year-old German kid who finished fifth at the 1991 Junior World 'Cross Championships—who never rode another 'Cross Worlds. He did, however, win the Tours of France and Switzerland: Jan Ullrich. He was just a regular teenager who started out as a 'cross rider in the winter and raced the road in the summer, chose the latter, and progressed as he went on to greater things. Need a bit more evidence? Look at Igor Arstaloa, the elite road world champ in 2003, who was pretty anonymous ten years previously. He placed twenty-ninth in the '93 Junior 'Cross Worlds, but he wasn't put off, and his persistence eventually paid large dividends.

To come through the teenage years and continue as a cyclist is an achievement in itself. Cycling does not have the glamorous image of many other sports, and not many people can make a good living from it compared to the mainstream sports that fill the television schedules. It is also too easy to fall in with what the majority does. During the school years, there is greater pressure to be one of the crowd or compete in a team sport, and not as much support for following an unusual individual sport like cyclocross. If you can make it through these years enjoying your cycling and learning what it's all about, and continue with a dedicated outlook, then the future for you will be bright.

Training for juvenile races should include a full range of sports. Within the context of cycling, the summers should be spent riding on the road or mountain bike, having fun, racing whatever and whenever you can, and building strength and experience as you simply ride your bike. Ride with a cycling club, go for rides with your friends on weekends, and take part in local evening races or weekend mountain-bike events. These are all great ways to get cycling experience without thinking of it as training.

You may also want to ride time trials, track, or circuit races if they are available during weekday evenings in your area. Short time trials

The next generation is here. Radomir Simunek Sr. is a 'cross legend with world titles as a junior, amateur, and professional over an amazing twenty-year career. The family name continues to shine as Radomir Jr. scores his first World Cup win in October 2006.

are perfect, as are most of the races that you find on a summer evening, since none of them are more than an hour in length. These races teach you how to ride fast—something you will have to do in cyclocross—and time trials will also teach you how to concentrate.

On weekends, try to ride a mix of races: some criteriums or circuit races as a juvenile and road races once you turn junior. These will teach you how to ride in a pack and how to brake and corner. Mountain-bike races will improve your bike-handling skills off-road, and at around 60 to 90 minutes in length they are longer than a 'cross race, so you will get a good conditioning workout.

In the winter, race as many weekends as you can. Many areas have local cyclocross races, some on Saturdays. By riding these, you can leave Sunday free for longer rides with your friends or cycling club, or maybe even for another race if there is one close by. During the week, do not train hard until you have recovered from your weekend's activities. As you will be at school, any training you do will be in the evenings, so make sure your bike has a good lighting system and that you can be seen.

Many areas have some kind of midweek training ride, usually attended by road racers keeping an edge on their winter fitness with a brisk ride. These are ideal for you, and they are much better (and safer) than training alone. If you have difficulty keeping up for the full distance, go as far as you can with the group until you get dropped, then ride home steadily. You will be able to gauge whether you are improving by seeing how far you get each week.

On other evenings, find some well-lighted grassland—either a floodlit sports field or some grass by a road—and practice your technique on your 'cross bike. Try to do this with a friend, if possible, to work on basic skills—mounting and dismounting, getting your feet in and out of the pedals quickly, and running with your bike for short stretches. You should also try to get into the habit of stretching regularly to keep your muscles flexible. You are still growing, and this will reduce the likelihood of your experiencing any growing pains due to contracted muscles. As you get older and increase your training load, you'll benefit greatly from the flexibility that stretching regularly will provide.

All of this, combined with school sports, will be adequate. Remember, your training should be progressive, and you will not see results overnight. Weight training should be avoided until you are fully mature, but circuit training and core stability work are great if you can fit them in, either at home or in the school gym.

Pay attention to your diet, and follow the guidelines in the section on nutrition. Try to avoid too much junk food and candy, and definitely do not ignore meals to fit in more training. At all times, it is important to eat regularly and sensibly, but even more so if you are still growing.

Road and Mountain-Bike Racing for Cyclocross International

A summer with regular road or mountain-bike racing, or a mix of the two, should figure in the program of every 'cross racer to improve strength, speed, and skill. Chances are good that you came into 'cross via the road bike or mountain bike anyway, so don't stop now—both types of riding complement 'cross riding and will help you develop 'cross skills.

If there is one discipline that forms the basis of conditioning for all others in cycling, it's road racing. Whether you're a 4,000-meter team pursuiter on the track or a 'cross pro, the need to condition your body and build strength by racing regularly on the road is paramount. If you haven't ridden the road in a past life, then you will probably be a lowly category racer. The majority of road races for these classes will be 40 to 60 miles, and you should try to race these whenever possible. Also race criteriums whenever you can; they require an effort that is very similar to the kind of effort required in cyclocross, with constant changes of pace into and out of corners. They will also teach you to ride fast in the corners close to the wheel in front, which is a required and transferable skill for your winter racing.

If you are a more experienced road rider, then you will be in a better position to sort out a more detailed road program. Again, ride criteriums whenever possible, and mix these with short-stage races and longer one-day races to build your strength. Unfortunately, changes in UCI regulations for road racing mean that composite teams are no longer possible for the majority of the better-quality stage races. At one time, individually sponsored or small-team 'cross riders were in demand to make up teams for a wide variety of stage races. Swiss star Beat Wabel, once a junior world champ and elite medalist who also placed in the top ten pretty much every year in the 1990s, said it changed his summer training when he could no longer race the Swiss stage races: "I would race the Tour of Romandie and the Tour of Switzerland on a composite team with the other Swiss individual pros and I would get such good form from them, it lasted for the winter." He added, "It also gave a good focus and great motivation for my summer as I had to train like hell because I knew it would be so hard to race at that level on the road; I could never have trained so hard if it was only for the winter. I also used to spend a couple of weeks in September before the 'cross season started doing kermesse racing in Belgium; that is also great preparation for a 'cross rider." And of course this is still possible. If you are European-based, consider creating your own mini stage races in the summer by racing back-to-back days of kermesse races in Belgium; there is certainly no lack of them, and it is very simple for an individual to do this.

Most 'cross riders make excellent road riders, but it doesn't work both ways. The good fitness and bike-handling skills common in 'cross transfer well to the requirements of road racing, but roadies riding 'cross usually suffer because their cardiovascular system cannot keep up—the demands of 'cross make them gasp. That is why so many roadies find cyclocross such an excellent form of training. 'Cross also improves their bike skills for the coming races on European roads, some of which resemble 'cross courses themselves!

If you have come into 'cross from a mountain-bike background, you may have been drawn to 'cross simply because you wanted to carry on racing off-road after the established mountain-bike season had finished. You probably even rode the early part of your 'cross career on the mountain bike until you realized that a 'cross bike was the faster option. Now that you're more into 'cross, don't neglect the mountain-bike races during the summer. Some of them, depending on location, are like riding a two-hour 'cross, and the majority will subject you to the kind of terrain and effort that will make a 'cross race seem like a ride in the park.

For the improvement of bike-handling skills and the training effect of racing for a prolonged time at a high heart rate, mountain-bike races are simply unbeatable—you could never subject yourself to the same stresses through training alone. But if you like to race a full season on a mountain bike in the summertime, you may be tempted to neglect the conditioning you need to get you through the winter. To remedy this situation, mix in some road racing, or at the very least, schedule blocks of quality endurance work into your training plan to get yourself in the best possible condition come October.

Rest and Recovery Revisited

We have already touched on the importance of rest in conjunction with training on a daily basis. However, it is important to incorporate rest as part of your plan for the entire year too.

Training in "cycles" of a number of weeks followed by a "rest" period gives you both a physical break and an equally important mental respite. Follow the recommendations regarding cycles provided in Chapter 4, and don't neglect the rest and recovery weeks. Toward the end of a training block, knowing you have only one more hard week, and then a break, can be a great motivating factor to work harder. It's a bit like counting down the last few intervals in a session. And your body needs the easier week to recover adequately and get ready for the next level.

To make an all-out effort fifty-two weeks a year is not possible or even preferable for even the most committed person. The recovery weeks within the phases are important, and occasional longer breaks are also important. Sometimes you need to lock the bike away and go do something else to stop yourself from going stale. For most riders, the best time to have a prolonged break is straight after the end of the season in February. This should give you a two- or three-week period of relative relaxation before pre-summer training camps start. Another break at summer's end is also advisable, but this one should not be quite as long as your spring break, as you are going into a racing phase.

Appropriate breaks and recovery time should keep you fresh and motivated all year-round. Having a rest week does not mean you can't get on your bike; it simply means you should not have a strictly regimented plan. If you don't feel like riding, don't go out. If the sun is shining and there's nothing you'd like more than a 3-hour ride, then do it. For a few days, the mental strain of watching the clock, waiting for the next session, and wondering if the rain will stop is lifted. Catch up on rest, go out a couple of nights, and switch off for a while. Physically, you won't lose too much, especially if you put in the occasional unstructured workout; you won't get fitter, though, so don't make it habit-forming! Mentally, the respites will do you a world of good, and you will enter the next phase of your training plan raring to go.

CHAPTER 6

Racing

All the efforts you put into your training regime—the hours you spend on your bike in all kinds of weather, the running, the weight training, the stretching, the core sessions, the attention to diet, the detailed attention to keeping your bike running sweetly, and all those early nights when you come home to get your rest while your friends are out partying—have a single aim: the race. Racing is what it's all about and why you do it. You may not take some races as seriously as others. Small, local races may be used as a means to an end, a training session to help prepare for a major race in the future. But even in the minor races, your race-day routine should be the same as for the big event, so that come the big day everything is just that—a routine.

Routine is all about organization. Routine means that you always know where to find something because you always put it back in the same place after it has been cleaned or used. Routine and organization go hand in hand, especially in a sport like cyclocross. In 'cross, sometimes you will have a dirty, messy day when you will have to use a lot more gear than you would for, say, a summer road race, and you will have to know exactly where each item is to find it quickly. Your own little routines make everything simple so that you can approach a race in a calm, focused manner. Your routine might well be broken: For example, you may find yourself racing abroad in a country where your normal pre-race meal is not available, or where supporting races mean

> ## WEATHER
>
> Having raced in the worst of conditions during a 'cross season gives me a much better state of mind when I am getting dressed for a road race in foul weather. I often enjoy the disappointment on the faces of my competitors as we set off for a 5-hour, 125-mile road race in cold rain.
>
> **MARK McCORMACK**

training times on the circuit vary from what you are used to. But if you are generally organized, then you won't be fazed by anything that is thrown at you outside of your normal routine.

It is impossible to put down on paper the "ideal" routine. Traveling times vary, as do race start times, so you must get to know what works best for you. The more race experience you get, the better you will be able to hone your routines to cover all the bases. However, there are some basic points that should be noted, so let's take a look at a "normal" race day.

Race Preparation

Preparation for a race actually starts long before race day: In a sense, it's what you've been doing all along. You've already done your best to train, you've already worked out your race taper, and you've already supplied your body with the right nutrients. So let's say you're down to the last few days before a race. What else can you do to make sure you are in top condition on race morning?

The final preparation for a Sunday race should start on Friday. Usually a relatively light training day, depending on your schedule, this is the day to sort out your equipment so that any problems can be rectified down at the bike shop on Saturday. Follow the recommendations for going over your bike in Chapter 2.

This is also the important night for sleep, so get an early night. Saturday may find you in a strange bed, if you need to travel to the race, and this—combined with restlessness as pre-race nerves start to take hold—might mean that a good night's sleep will escape you. If you sleep well on Friday, you will be fine on Sunday.

Train on Saturday as you normally would, with either a pre-ride on the circuit or a 60- to 90-minute road ride, with some short, sharp efforts to spark the systems and remind your body what it will be doing the next day. One important Saturday goal is pre-race fueling. If you get this right the day before, then on race day you will not have to try to cram a bit more food into a body that is being ravaged by nerves, which tend to suppress appetite. Graze during the day Saturday, make sure you fuel properly during and after your training ride, and pay some attention to the evening meal. The aim here is to top up your energy stores, so the meal should be high in carbohydrates—ideally pasta, rice, baked potatoes, or bread with perhaps chicken, salad, or vegetables. Keep hydrated with plenty of plain water. As for alcohol, avoid anything more than a glass of wine with dinner. Leave a few hours between this meal and bedtime so you can relax and digest it; don't try to sleep on a full stomach.

RACE-DAY MEALS

If your main race starts at around, say, 2:00 P.M., with a supporting race at midday, then eat breakfast at around 8:00–8.30 A.M., and then have a pre-race snack no later than 11:00 A.M. Combine breakfast with your snack if the race start is midday or earlier.

For breakfast, eat whatever you are used to. Cereal, muesli, fruit, or toast with honey or jam is fine. Keep this meal light and nutritious;

avoid anything too heavy, and definitely steer clear of fried food, such as bacon and fried eggs. Anything else pre-race should also be light but high in carbohydrates—for example, a small pasta dish, omelet, or scrambled eggs and toast, which are all quick, easy, tasty, and nutritious. It's important to learn how your body responds to different foods during regular training weeks; then, on race day, you can go with foods that you've already tried and tested. At the same time, be flexible if your first preference is not available. There's no need to go overboard and fill yourself up; you are only racing for an hour, and you can easily store enough glycogen in your muscles and blood to fuel a high-intensity effort for that length of time.

Do not consume a lot of sugar or candy on a race morning; complex carbs, which release energy into the bloodstream at a slower but more consistent rate than simple sugars, are much better at this time of day, and you'll be getting these in your cereal and toast. If pre-race nerves or a tight travel schedule means that you cannot get a meal down, then use sports drinks and snack bars. Drinks based around glucose polymers and specific sports bars by SiS, PowerBar, and Clif Bar are all ideal, as are supermarket-brand grain and soft muesli or granola bars. Above all, do not eat anything within two hours of the race start, except for perhaps a carbohydrate gel washed down with a few mouthfuls of your sports drink when you have just a few minutes to go.

WHAT TO TAKE TO A RACE

Differences in weather over a 'cross season can mean big variations in the amount of clothing you will need on race days. However, you must be prepared for all eventualities with clothing to suit all conditions. Do not forget a good supply of plastic bags. You can put your wet, muddy clothing in these to keep them separate from dry items. Shoe bags are good for keeping all the gloves, mitts, beanies, caps, neck warmers, and so on separate and easy to find.

RACE-DAY CHECKLIST

Warm-Up Kit

- Shoes
- Overshoes
- Socks
- Shorts
- Base layers: short-sleeved and long-sleeved
- Short-sleeved and long-sleeved jerseys
- Bib tights
- Training jackets
- Vest
- Thermal jacket
- Rain jacket
- Training hat or beanie (which should be on your head every time your helmet isn't!)
- Fleece neck warmer
- Gloves and track mitts
- Tear-off tights or leg warmers
- Eyewear

Race Kit (separate from above)

- Helmet
- Shoes
- Socks
- Skinsuit
- Arm warmers
- Base layer
- Leg warmers
- Knee warmers
- Gloves
- Track mitts
- Cotton and waterproof caps
- Chest protector
- Eyewear and selection of lenses for all conditions
- Two towels: one for embrocation, one for after race
- Shower gel and shampoo
- Sports wash and flannels for removing embrocation
- Embrocation box
- Safety pins
- Shoelaces or spare shoe fastenings
- Spare studs and spikes for shoes
- Bottles with pre- and post-race drinks
- Bars, gels, and snacks
- Small first-aid kit
- Racing license
- Plastic bags
- Flask

(continues)

If you are planning to travel abroad to race, add a passport to the list. And if you're traveling much distance at all, you'll be spending large amounts of time sitting in a car, in a hotel room, and possibly in various airports. To make life a little more bearable, take along the following:

- Travel kettle
- Box containing tea, coffee, chocolate, powdered milk, sugar, spoon, and so on
- iPod
- Laptop
- Books and magazines
- Travel plug for overseas electrical outlets
- Four-way master plug extension lead

The last item is a must. After all, when was the last time you were in a hotel room that had enough wall sockets to charge all of your electrical gadgets?

THE WARM-UP

Aim to arrive at the race with plenty of time to spare; a minimum of two hours before the race is ideal. Don your warm-up clothing and, on your spare bike, start inspecting the circuit. Your helper should also be looking at the circuit, perhaps walking a lap. He or she will be looking for the pit areas, availability of water, changing rooms, registration area, and toilets.

Aim to complete three or four laps during your warm-up. The first two laps should be slow with plenty of looking and learning. Don't simply ride around with your teammates catching up on the gossip; sort out your best lines and decide which gears to use in different sections. Think about various ways to approach the course; that is, look "out of the box" and away from the lines that everyone else is follow-

COURSE CONDITIONS

You never know what a course is going to throw at you. Thick peanut-butter mud, energy-sucking sand pits, tricky off-camber sections, hellaciously long run-ups, and death-defying descents are all part of the program. You really need to be ready for anything.

Whatever the conditions, you must remain level-headed in a cyclocross race because it's more than likely that you will crash, trip over a barrier, slip a pedal, or wash out on a corner at some point during a race. Weak-minded riders crash, get flustered, and go on to have a bad race. Strong-minded riders also make plenty of mistakes, but they put small mishaps behind them and focus on riding smoothly and aggressively. These are the riders that always finish well.

BRANDON DWIGHT

ing. In particular, look for alternative routes around trees and see if there are longer lines that may seem out of the way but could have a better surface or allow for a better transition, enabling you to carry more speed into the next section. Remember, as long as it's between the tapes that mark the circuit, you can ride anywhere. These alternatives will become especially useful if you find yourself with company toward the end of the race, or if you start lapping the tail-enders, as you can take your "secret" alternative route to make an attack or pass someone without getting held up.

Pay particular attention to the ground conditions and any muddy sections of the course that might get worse as the race goes on. Perhaps there is a longer route available that is drier. If you have done a thorough course inspection before the race, you can be flexible during the race, knowing you have studied all the options. Your inspection should include the starting area and the first section of the course, especially the first corner off the road at the start, as you will be traveling significantly faster then than on subsequent laps. If there is a small starting loop that is not included on every lap, check that out as well. Look for the fastest transition from the road to the off-road section. Check for any holes, deep gravel, or ruts that could take you off your ideal line, or anything else that could affect your perfect start—or that could be a hazard as you motor down the road at 45 kilometers per hour with a hundred riders behind you, trusting your every move. Decide on the best place to position yourself at the starting line, if you get an option. If the start is not gridded or if the area is narrow, you can always position your helper on the line with your start bike sometime before the beginning of the race to ensure that you get your spot. Meanwhile, you can continue to warm up on your spare bike.

Finish your training on the course about an hour before the race starts. Have one last drink if you need one, and then head for the warmth of the changing rooms to change into race clothing and make your final preparations; this is the time to apply your embrocation if you use it. Make sure you do not head back out to the start in just your skinsuit; put on some warm tops and your tear-off tights or leg warmers. Now, on your best (starting) bike go for a warm-up on the road. This should be for 15 to 20 minutes. As you warm up, you can increase the effort through the training zones until you finish working pretty hard in Z4.

If you prefer to warm up on a home trainer, then you may be able to place it by the start area or by your car or team area. If it is raining or there is a cold wind blowing, look for a sheltered area.

The actual warm-up should be similar to the one recommended above for a road warm-up. Take around 20 minutes to warm up, gradually increasing the effort, and add in some short, 10- to 15-second bursts to finish.

Arrive at the starting area in good time, and do a few start efforts down the road. If you have your helper positioned on the line to keep your spot, then you can spend the final minutes slowly circling, keep-

A trainer can be the ideal warm-up tool.

ing warm, and focusing on the job at hand. Keep your extra clothing on as long as possible; the object is to keep warm so that you are ready for a violent starting effort.

The Race

Compared to road racing, where tactics and race strategy can play a large part in the outcome of the race—and the fittest person does not necessarily win—cyclocross tends to be much more straightforward. Barring accidents, the best person is usually first across the line. However, this does not mean that tactics cannot be employed. In races where the leading contenders are very similar in ability, such as World Championship events, riders who use their heads as well as their legs will come out on top.

Recently, with the Belgian domination of world 'cross, the World Championships have been a showcase of teamwork, but not always just one nationality against another, as the Belgians don't usually relish the idea of helping each other. It has become fairly common to see a leading group of four or five Belgians representing a couple of the big teams working the team angle, while an interloper or two from other nations hang in there hoping to pick up the scraps if they get it wrong. They invariably don't, though! So with, say, Vervecken and Wellens from Fidea up against Nys and Vanthourenhout from Rabobank, it becomes an intriguing battle of four Belgians from two opposing trade teams. Add into the mix a Dutchman, say Groenendaal from Rabobank, and a Czech, say Dlask from Fidea, and there is another dimension.

Does team loyalty outweigh personal ambition or national pride? It has become apparent in situations such as this in recent years that the trade team card usually trumps the national team one; after all, it's just one day a year when these racers put on their national uniforms, whereas their trade teams pay them all year. While fellow Belgians might not ride in support of each other if they are on rival teams, they tend not to actively ride against each other. In the scenario above, if Dlask attacks, then it's down to a Belgian to chase, but Wellens, say, would leave it to a Rabobank Belgian to do the majority of the work while he just followed, then if Dlask came back to the group he could attack himself. If that were the case, then another Belgian would never bring him back by actively chasing (although it has happened—ask Vervecken about Poprad in 1999 and what he thought of Mario De Clerq chasing him down on the last lap and leaving him with the silver medal!), and it's unlikely that a trade teammate of Wellens's from another nation would be seen to work hard to stop him from winning. So it's actually not a bad situation to be in; a non-Fidea rider from a nation other than Belgium would have to lead the chase, and that might be pretty hard to organize! It can be complicated, but it also certainly leads to some interesting racing.

Modern 'cross at the top levels no longer sees the "horses for courses" riders who were around a few years ago—that is, racers who tended to specialize in certain types of courses. All riders have their personal preferences about circuits and weather conditions, and there are always riders around who will excel in one extreme or another—in heavy mud or on ice, for example—but generally, the best riders are all-rounders who can shine on all types of courses.

It is important not to get into a situation where you think that certain conditions do not suit you; if you start to think this way, then every time you encounter these conditions you will be psychologically beaten before you start. If you are especially gifted as a runner, or prefer to race on ice, then by all means use this to your advantage. But work on your weaknesses and become a good all-round rider rather than a specialist. By riding to your strengths and limiting your losses on your weaknesses—and by knowing your competitors' strengths and weaknesses—you will have far more success than you would by just blindly hammering away from start to finish in the hope that you will win.

That said, it is no use working out your race-winning move if you are nowhere near the front of the race when you get a chance to use it. Good starting strategies are essential.

THE START

Although the starts of cyclocross races may not be as difficult as they used to be before all races began on roads with gridded lineups, a good start will still give you a psychological advantage. Once you're off to a good start, you can concentrate on the rest of the race knowing you are in a favorable position. You will be aware of who is up near the front, you will have a clear run around the circuit, and you will not lose time fighting your way past slower rivals.

A bad start, especially on a circuit with a number of narrow sections that cause bottlenecks, can be frustrating and can damage your

As you can see from this shot of a race start, the effort level is high and commitment is absolute as everyone tries to hit the first off-road section at the front.

chances. The usual response to a bad start is panic: You work too hard to get to the front too quickly, try passing riders where the course won't permit it, and make mistakes. You probably crash a few times, and the great job you did getting psyched up before the race start is wasted as you lose concentration and give up the fight.

If you are unlucky enough to have a ranking that gives you a poor gridding, or you actually have a poor start from a reasonable start position—and poor is anytime you lose places from your start position—it is important to remain calm and concentrate on gradually working your way back up to the front. Remember, you have an hour of racing to get back up there. If you put in a blistering two laps, the chances are high that you will simply blow up and spend the rest of the race trying to recover. It's not the end of the world. There may be twenty or thirty riders in front of you, but on early laps, if everyone is

still together, you may only be 20 seconds off the lead. If you have prepared yourself properly before the race, warmed up well, reconnoi-
tered the start area and the first part of the circuit, and can concentrate
on the job at hand, then your start should not let you down.

Practice during training should mean that your foot goes in the
pedal first time, every time. Start in a gear that's not too big or too
small. Your first pedal revolution should not come around so fast that
it makes pedal pickup difficult or makes the free pedal spin. But you
should also be able to accelerate fast for the first two or three revs to
get some space. When your foot is in and you've got the revs up, shift
up, get out of the saddle, and go for it!

Be aware of the riders around you—if there are riders in front, look
for gaps to go through. Never look down or lose concentration; always
look up, and be aware of "waves" in the bunch so you can take advantage of the gaps they create. At this time, there is no real need to hit
the front, unless there is a narrow section coming up. Sit near the
front, ideally among the first five or six riders, so you can keep an eye
on what is going on and follow any moves. Try to settle into a rhythm
as quickly as possible.

If your start didn't go as planned and you find yourself farther back
in the field, then it's even more crucial for you to concentrate. Save energy, but if the opportunity comes along and a gap suddenly opens in
front of you, make the most of it and make short, sharp efforts to move
up. Keep your head up and be aware of who is around you; if there are
some fast wheels around that you can follow, then so much the better.

RACE STRATEGY

Presuming your start has been a good one and you find yourself in the
leading group, what tactics can you employ to ensure a victory? This
is where your knowledge of the circuit, your understanding of your
own strengths and weaknesses, and your awareness of your opponents'
strengths and weaknesses will come into play.

Don't expect road sections will be a chance to recover! As you can see from this shot of Roger Hammond putting the pressure on, a road section is an ideal place to turn up the pressure or to close a gap if the riders in front start to ease up slightly.

If you are a strong technical rider, runner, or hurdler, then you should ride at the front and wear down the opposition by applying a bit of pressure each time you get to a section that plays on your strengths. Don't throw in any full-on attacks at this stage of the race unless you are confident that you can ride the rest of the race alone. If you are capable, running sections are a good place to attack, because the slipstreaming effect while running is negligible. It is therefore of no benefit physically for someone to "sit" on you as it is on the riding sections. Another good place to make your move is on any obstacle or part of the circuit that you can ride, but for which your rivals must dismount. If you are confident, say, of riding a bank that everybody else is running, think about using this to your advantage. On early laps, go ahead and run it; then, at a time you choose for your attack, you will have the element of surprise when you stay on your bike and attack out of the obstacle.

In your pre-race inspection, you will have found any faster lines along the course. Again, unless you are out in front on your own, do not use them all the time. Follow your rivals around the obvious but slower sections, and then attack just before you reach the section with the alternate route—if possible, when the gap behind you is big enough that other riders will not see you and follow your lead.

Most cyclocross tactics presuppose that everybody is racing as an individual, but in reality, most people ride for a team. If you have teammates in the race, tactics can be employed that are similar to those used on the road. If you find yourself with a teammate and one of you is able, attack and leave the rest to chase you with your teammate sitting in. The classic combination in the United States in recent seasons has been the Kona Team pairing of Ryan Trebon and Barry Wicks. One of the only teams with two riders capable of riding in the front group, they have employed this tactic on numerous occasions with great success.

It's pretty simple to execute, but difficult to police: One attacks, the other follows, and if caught, the other can attack immediately and leave the teammate to sit on the chasers. Eventually, chasers will be unable to keep making the efforts required, and one of the two teammates will be able to stay clear. When one of them manages to escape the clutches of the group, the other rider can still help by leading the group through any narrow sections, but not at full speed. This will effectively break up the chase and slow the group, allowing the gap to widen.

So, what if you are the one being attacked? How can you stop what has been described above from happening to you? First, know your opponent. If you know someone's strength, then make sure you are first into his or her preferred section so that you can lead at your own pace. With a bike on your shoulder it's not too hard to keep somebody behind you. But though it may be easy to keep the others behind you when you're losing time on slippery switchback corners, watch out for them the moment you exit the section, as this is an excellent time for them to try to get clear.

If someone is riding a bank you have to run, approach it in the lead and take it at your own pace. The other racer will need a clear run to ride it faster than you can run it, so take the opportunity to break up his or her rhythm. In addition, watch your opponents as they go through the pits. Are they taking a clean bike every lap? Are their bike changes good ones? Is it worth skipping a bike change to attack as they go into the pit? This will depend on the state of the course and the state of your bike, but bear it in mind—it might be just what they were not expecting you to do!

If you still find yourself in company at the end of the race and are resigned to a sprint finish, then make sure you are leading into the final obstacle, whether it is the last bend or a dismount, and lead out. But you need to think about this a few laps out, as the last opportunity to move up could easily be some distance from the finish. You need to work it out with at least two laps to go. It's rare for a cyclocross race to have a very long finishing straight where you can employ road-sprint tactics, and in the event of a sprint, the one who leads out usually is successful.

STRATEGY

I have two race strategies. The first is damage control. When I am in a nationally ranked race and I know a top-15 finish is going to be a very tall order, this is my strategy. I try not to be too ambitious at the start—it's fruitless to attempt to stay with riders I have no business riding with. It's better to start somewhat aggressively and not go over my limit, and then slowly pick off riders throughout the race.

My second strategy stems from the motto "second place is the first loser." I know this sounds a little cocky, but if I don't win, then I know

I can do better, and this motivates me to train hard and go for it in the next race. I've won two cyclocross races in ten years of racing, so you get the point.

There are many times during a cyclocross race when you are completely by yourself and team or group tactics are not an option. Usually this means you are trying desperately to crawl back to the group in front of you or not get sucked up by the group chasing you down. In these situations it's best to not lose your cool and to ride as smoothly as possible. Ride aggressively on all straightaway sections because chances are good that the groups in front or behind you are not going as fast on these sections—no one wants to take a strong pull at the front of their respective group. If you corner smoothly, clean the barriers, and ride smart you just might catch the group in front. Slipping out on one corner or flailing over a barrier will cost you valuable time.

If you are lucky enough to race with teammates, a race can be really fun. You can take a flyer off the front, making all the others in the group work to catch you while your teammates sit on the back of the pack in the draft, saving energy. Once the group catches you, a well-rested teammate can take another flyer off the front. Once again, the group needs to work to catch your teammate. This can go on over and over again, but eventually a rider will get away because the group is so exhausted and no one wants to chase down the race leader.

Team tactics can also be used by riders who aren't on the same team. Maybe you have a friend or a fellow racer in your group whom you respect, and the two of you decide before or during the race to work together on an escape. In these situations you are teammates until the last lap, and then it's time to battle each other to the finish. Once, in a small regional race, I escaped from the lead group with former national champion Marc Gullickson. We worked together throughout the entire event to keep the chase group from catching us. On the last lap, he dropped me like a bad habit.

BRANDON DWIGHT

After the Race

After the race, the most important thing in the short term is getting back into some warm, dry clothing. If possible, have someone meet you at the finish with a clean jersey and hat so you can be warm and presentable—should you be required to hang around talking to the press or for a presentation. If you are not needed, do not stand about; instead, go for a 5-minute cool-down, then head for the changing rooms and a hot shower. Make sure you leave the changing rooms feeling nice and warm, with dry hair, warm clothes, and a hat. By doing so, you are already preparing for the next race by taking good care of yourself and aiding your recovery.

The next most important concern after a race (or indeed a training session) should be refueling as quickly as possible. Your muscles are best able to replenish their glycogen stores during the first 30 minutes following exercise, when eating is the last thing you feel like doing. Take it in liquid form—recovery drinks are quick, clean, palatable, and easily absorbed. The ideal recovery drink or snack should contain around 10 to 20 grams of protein and between 30 to 50 grams of carbohydrate. Use one of the drinks specifically designed for the purpose, such as Re-Go from SiS, or simply make your own smoothie with low-fat milk and a banana. If you make it in the morning and take it with you, you can have the bottle or thermos in your bag to drink in the changing room.

Race Promotion for the First-Timer

Maybe you're tired of having to travel to find races. Or you've been to races in other cities and towns and think it would be great fun to have a race in your own community. It could stir up local interest in the sport and generate some publicity—and perhaps new members—for your club. If so, go for it. There can never be too many races on the calendar, and a 'cross is probably the easiest kind of bike race to promote, so round up some friends and teammates and put on a race.

All the big races out there started small, so follow suit. Race organizers have to grow with their events, so start with a Saturday afternoon affair for the locals. Before you know it, you could be staging the national championships or an international event.

First off, find a venue. This could be the park you train in, your kids' school sports field, or the woods behind the local trash dump—anywhere with enough varied terrain to allow you to set out a circuit of 1 or 2 miles. But if your site has a few facilities attached to it, then so much the better. Sports centers and schools are favorite locations. They have changing facilities, rooms to use as headquarters for registration and results, larger rooms for prize presentations, bathrooms, space for first-aid stations and medical control (to follow antidoping rules), even parking for the hordes of competitors and spectators who will show up. Even though you are starting small, if you can start with facilities that would be adequate for a larger race, you will be looking ahead to the time when your annual race becomes a major event. The grounds of these buildings usually comprise grassland, steep banks, asphalt paths, and rougher ground that will suit a race circuit. The only other requirement is a little imagination.

But don't forget the practical aspects of putting on a race, such as discussing your plans thoroughly with the property owners or the school or park officials. It's best to present your plans in writing, after an initial discussion, and get written permission to carry them out, in order to avoid misunderstandings. Take care of the legal considerations—insurance matters, for example—and make sure you have a signed liability waiver from every participant to reduce the likelihood of legal problems if there are injuries. Make sure you arrange for appropriate first aid and medical help. And if you're expecting to use the same course the next year, be sure to keep up a good working relationship with the property owners—for example, make sure the site is cleaned up and put back into perfect condition when the race is over. It's worth going over race plans with an attorney to make sure you have all the bases covered. Have him or her read the agreement you will have with the property owners as well as your liability waiver, for starters.

Once you've arranged for the basics, think about how to set up the circuit. Even a boring piece of grassy meadow can be transformed with a few marking posts and a length of tape. If your race venue cannot help out with course setup, then ask the local authority or construction company for a loan of equipment. Remember, marking pins need to be wood or plastic, not metal.

If there are enough natural obstacles on the course to force the riders off their bikes up to a maximum of six times a lap (to conform with UCI rules if you grow to become a bigger event)—up short steep run-ups, over a ditch, and so on—then leave your course as is. If the area you choose is relatively free of anything but grass, then you are going to have to construct some obstacles. Again, UCI rules dictate only one set of hurdles per lap, and these need to be a maximum height of 40 centimeters (15.75 in.). You can have two only, 4 meters (about 13 ft.) apart, and they need to be the full width of the circuit and solid enough so that if they are rideable, they will not collapse if hit or stepped on. Also, mark them tightly on each side so that they cannot be ridden around. Play around with the location of these hurdles. You could put them at the bottom of a slope to make a run-up, or set them on a flat, fast section of course to encourage the skillful riders to try to bunny-hop them.

Mark out a pit area, preferably on a running section so that the riders are already off their bikes (which makes bike changing easier) and near a water supply. The area on the right side of the circuit should be wide enough to accommodate mechanics and spare bikes.

For the start area, one option is to mark out a flat piece of ground just off the circuit that is at least 6 meters (20 ft.) wide, to allow for the riders to be gridded. Or you could find a long road section that leads into the circuit proper. Try to allow the field time to spread out before they hit the first obstacle or bottleneck; most riders hate queuing on the opening lap.

At your finish line, allow room for the judges, and provide some covering for them, if possible; results sheets drenched in rain do not make for easy reading. If the finish can be down a barriered road, then so much the better for spectators, sprint finishes, and photographers.

Don't forget when setting out the course that it is a cyclocross race, not a mountain-bike event. The emphasis should be on the speed, skill, and strength of the riders. Do not include any extended sections of singletrack, as it causes too many problems with lapped riders; avoid extreme climbs or descents that favor the attributes of a mountain bike; and skip sections of ground that will turn your 'cross into a footrace if the rains arrive.

Once you have figured out the location, circuit, and course design, try not to keep it a secret: Take it to the people. A race in Europe tends to be based around a village or small town so there is a captive audience. You often see small posters or flyers for races in the local bars and supermarkets. It's rare that they are held a long way from civilization, so it's relatively easy to attract a crowd. If you can get the right venue to attract good numbers of spectators, you will find it easier to get local businesses and the local media involved, and you will attract sponsorship, which in turn will have an impact on the quality of riders you attract. The result is that your race will grow, and everybody benefits.

CHAPTER 7

The Role of the Mechanic

As soon as your cyclocross becomes even slightly serious, you will appreciate the need for a spare bike, and as soon as you have a spare bike you will need a capable pair of hands to take care of it for you at the races. Any race on a muddy circuit will leave you at a considerable disadvantage if you try to compete on the same bike for the whole event. As the laps go by, your bike will get heavier and heavier, your tires and wheels will jam up with mud, and your gears will start jumping as the sprockets get clogged with mud, leaves, and grass. Once you have a spare to hop onto, your pit buddy becomes a crucial part of "Team You"!

Your first spare bike will probably be an old training bike or even a road bike—simply something to do a lap on every so often while somebody cleans your best bike. As you progress, you will end up with two identical bikes, and on those really bad days you might want to change them every lap. In this way, you will always be on an immaculate bike as your helper cleans the other one.

This chapter is for the benefit of your pit crew—your helper, mechanic, manager, massage therapist, coach, adviser, and gofer. Whether it's spouse or sweetheart, parent or friend, teammate or professional mechanic, you cannot do without an assistant, so it is important that he or she become involved and learn what is required to help your races run smoothly. As you improve, so will your assistant—and if you become a winning team, then you will share equally in the joys of victory.

After a relatively unglamorous racing career that ended early after an injury, I started helping out some of the friends I had trained and raced with and became their pit-guy. As I was no longer able to satiate my competitive urges on the bike, I changed my focus and soon wanted to be the best bike cleaner out there. Just as I had studied the stars while pre-riding circuits to see what I could learn from them as a rider, so I studied the mechanics. I watched them and learned from them, noticing what they took to the races, and particularly to the pits, which workstands they used, which rain pants they wore, which buckets they had, and especially which brushes they used on the bike (the ultimate cleaning brush *is* the Holy Grail of 'cross mechanics!). I discovered new routines to make my job easier and more efficient, and I refined my tools and equipment as I went along. The great thing was that this was all happening as the riders I was working with grew in stature and ability. I was never a novice working with professionals; we learned together, and it was a rewarding time as I filled the void that not being able to compete had left.

Equipment

For life in the pits, the first thing to take care of is your clothing. You are going to get wet, cold, and dirty, so dress accordingly. Waterproof footwear and trousers are a must, with plenty of warm clothing on your upper body and a waterproof jacket if the weather is bad. It's not a bad idea to wear something that identifies you at a glance to your rider as he or she approaches a pit with sixty mechanics in it. A team

Life in the pits.

jacket works if the weather is okay, but consider what might serve the purpose when it turns cold and wet.

Regular gloves are impractical, as your hands will frequently be either wet or in water; rubber gloves or the disposable, tight-fitting latex work gloves that car mechanics use are good if it is really cold. Alternatively, when the riders are getting ready and putting embrocation on their legs, you can rub some of their cream into your hands, or simply do their legs for them. With some of the hotter embrocations on the market, it can almost be a pleasure to put your hands into an icy bucket of water to cool them down. Your footwear needs to have a reasonably good tread; pits can become muddy, slippery places. And you may end up in streams fetching water or cleaning bikes, so plan accordingly.

The next thing you will need is a bike-cleaning kit, and this comes down to three possible options. At the big races, such as the World Championships, the World Cups, and the like, the organizers are required to provide pressure washers in the pit area for general use, so option one at these events is to use the neutral jet wash. The downside of this option is the number of mechanics versus the number of jet washers provided. You invariably have to wait in line and/or fight for your turn. The second option is to take your own pressure washer with you and be self-sufficient. The best pressure washers on the market are the Karcher K3300GS and any of the smaller ones from Honda, all gasoline-powered cleaners that cost about the same as a good set of wheels.

A cleaner, on its own, is pretty easy to get to the pits, as it can be wheeled; the issue is how to get a water supply for it. It is unlikely there will be water on tap in the pit, so you need to figure out a different solution. I use a barrel or water butt that has a hose-lock connection at the bottom for simple hookup to the cleaner, and then take separate water containers that can be filled at the closest source. You should be able to find the water barrel at your local garden center.

Now something like the Karcher can knock out water at 350 liters (90 gallons) an hour, which is some quantity to be carrying around, so consider how much you will need and learn to clean bikes using as little as you can get away with. Nothing is worse than trying to apologize to a rider mid-race because you have run out of water and can't give him or her a clean bike!

While on the subject of pressure washers, I should mention that just recently a couple of manufacturers have introduced smaller models that are powered from your car cigarette lighter and have a small reservoir built in to hold water. These are ideal for giving your bike a quick cleaning after a training lap or before you pack it into the car after a race. If you fill it with hot water when you leave for the race, it can be great for washing with if there are no changing rooms. They are cheap,

Bike stand, tools, water, brushes, and lube; with the addition of some spare wheels you are all set for an hour in the pits, and if you can color-coordinate your boots with your tools and buckets, then you really are a pro!

small, portable, easy to set up in a couple of minutes, and perfect for reducing the amount of mud that travels home with you.

The third option is to use the faithful bucket. I take three—stable, rectangular ones that fit inside each other. The top one carries all the bits I will need during the race, leaving two to fill with water if there is none available near the pit. These are also useful to have around the car for cleaning shoes before the race and bikes and legs after the finish. Incidentally, the Pedros "Super Pit Kit" bucket is a wonderful bit of kit for any mechanic, as it has a screw-top lid to keep all the bits and pieces you need safe or, if you actually carry water in it, to keep it from sloshing out.

MECHANIC MUST-HAVES

Along with your bike-cleaning equipment, you need to have a small bag of tools with you in the pits (a shoe bag or fanny pack is best). This bag should contain the following items:

- Spare gear and brake cable
- Allen wrenches (3, 4, 5, 6, and 8 mm)
- Open-ended/ring wrenches (7, 8, 9, and 10 mm)
- Crank-bolt wrench (if not Allen-key type)
- Pliers
- Chain riveter
- Small screwdriver for gear adjustment
- Insulation tape
- Scissors

With so many multitools now available, it is almost possible to pack the above into a couple of pocket-sized tools; check out your local bike shop for options.

You will also need cleaning and lubing items:

- Sponges, medium-size (hard sponges are best as they do not fall apart on spokes or cable ends)
- Brushes (small, stiff ones for scrubbing tires and pedals)
- Dry cloths (for drying the bike after washing; cut-up old T-shirts are best)
- Thin screwdriver or an extra spoke (for cleaning between sprockets when they are really clogged up)
- Spray lubricant (both thick and thin, depending on the course and the weather conditions)

If you are using a pressure washer you will also need to have the following:

- A bike stand to hold or support the bike while you spray it
- Spare fuel in a safe, sealed container

Finally, you will need to have spare wheels with you. Normally just one pair is sufficient in case of a puncture, but you could bring two pairs if you want to have different tire choices available to suit the conditions you find on the course. A mud-tread option is nice if the weather looks changeable or if the course could deteriorate and become slippery.

Setting Up Your Pit Area

The style of pits has changed over the past few years. They are now located off the racing circuit with an entrance and exit, and there is a pit lane where the mechanics stand with the bikes. In major races, there can only be one pit, but this has to cover two sections of the course (a "double pit"). It is divided into boxes, which are allocated to the teams or countries at the race briefing, usually the evening before the race. You set up camp in your box, and you have to change bikes from your area only. This rule was implemented to reduce the number of bikes required to be competitive. Racers now have simply the bike that is being raced and one spare in a pit, but they can change a bike either for cleaning or for a mechanical problem.

In smaller races there is usually a single pit area, but occasionally pit areas are not provided and you can choose where you want to set up. While the riders are training on the course prior to the race, take a walk around and locate the pit, work out how to get there from the parking lot with all your gear, and find the closest water source. If at this time you are setting up your pressure washer, consider where the water is going to go; you will not be popular if you're spraying water into the crowd or onto passing riders. Give yourself some room to move around in and do your job without interfering with other pit crews.

If there is enough mud on the circuit to clog up the bike, and coming into the pit is not a hindrance to your rider, then it is best to change bikes each lap. It is easier to clean a bike after a single lap than to wait two or three laps and let it get really bad. It might not then be possible to get it completely clean within a lap, and if on that lap your rider punctures, he or she is not going to be able to get a clean spare. Changing every lap also means the rider is always on a clean, fast bike.

If you do decide to change every lap, you have to be confident that you can get enough water for, say, ten cleans. This means you'll need to find a water source, be it tap, stream, or pond. I have even cleaned a bike in a puddle. It was nowhere near the circuit, but the race was muddy and there was no water to be found anywhere. Following each bike change, I would jump on the bike and pedal to my puddle in the middle of nowhere, clean it, and return just in time to change again. After that race, I had probably ridden the same distance as the rider; at least it felt that way, what with flat-out riding and cleaning for one hour. But as it took most of the race for the other mechanics to figure out what I was up to, and since I had a clean bike while they were trying to scrape off the worst of the mud with their hands, I could feel a certain sense of achievement.

If there is no water about, or you are tied to a pit with nothing close by, you will have to resort to your buckets, which you can fill somewhere and leave in the pit before the start. You will simply have to be more sparing with what you use.

Bike Changing

Bike changing is certainly worth practicing with your rider before the season gets under way, so that both of you understand the different methods of bike changing before finding yourselves in a race situation.

There are two ways to hand a bike up: straight onto the rider's shoulder, if the pit is situated on a section of course the riders have to run or at the bottom of a run-up, or on the ground, if the pit is situated on a riding section.

Whichever method is used, the rider must first drop the bike he is using. Ideally, he should hand it to someone, but if no spare hands are available, he should drop it to the side of the course where it will not interfere with the riders behind him. Many a rider has slung his bike down in the middle of the course in front of his opponents, only to see them simply run over it, bending wheels as they go!

But cyclocross rules state that no part of the circuit may be covered without a bike. The rider must therefore make sure she is only a step or two away from her helper when she drops the bike that is ready for

Erwin Vervecken gets a clean machine.

cleaning. All major races have commissaires in charge of the pits, and they are quick to notice riders running without a bike. Once is a warning; twice is disqualification.

If the clean bike is being handed up on the ground for a rider who is ready to jump straight onto it, the helper should have it in the correct gear for the following section of the circuit, with the cranks parallel to the ground and the right pedal facing forward. The helper should hold it by the bars and saddle, then let go of the bars as the rider grabs them, then push the bike by the saddle to help the rider keep his momentum.

If the situation dictates a bike on the shoulder, the helper should hold the bike in the air by the seat tube and handlebars, with the bars slightly over to the left if the rider carries the bike with her arm under the down tube. As the rider runs through the pit, the helper should run a few steps alongside her and place the bike on the rider's shoulder. It will take some practice for the rider to let the mechanic do this. The rider's natural reaction is to try to take the bike from the helper before it is on her shoulder. If the mechanic lets go with the bike unbalanced, the rider will have to juggle it, upsetting her rhythm, before she can get it on his shoulder correctly.

The main problem with bike changing occurs when the pit area is too small or too congested for easy maneuvering. On early laps before the field has strung out, you can find sixty mechanics all trying to get in a position to first see, then service, their riders. In this situation, it is imperative to make sure there is someone to catch the discarded bike, as there simply will be nowhere to put it.

Cooperation among mechanics can make life in the pits a lot easier. Remember that the race is among the riders—there is nothing to gain by an aggressive attitude in the pits. If your rider has already passed or has not yet arrived, stand back out of the way until he does arrive. Find out who is providing pit-crew help to the riders closest to yours, and spread out a bit to make sure both of you are able to be in position at the moment of bike changing.

Bike Cleaning

Once your rider has successfully changed bikes, you will probably have about 6 minutes before she reappears, expecting an immaculately clean bike for the next lap. Three minutes spent panicking reduces your cleaning time, so keep calm, stick to a routine, and all will be well.

Cleaning technique depends on two factors: which of the three options you have chosen as a cleaning method, and your water supply. If you are all set for using a pressure washer, hook the bike onto your stand, start the washer, and start cleaning, doing the wheels first. Direct the blast onto the tread, and this will start the wheel spinning; you'll get wet and dirty as the spinning wheel gets clean. Mud will also

While a work stand is not required, a jet wash definitely is!

spin off the tire onto the frame during this step, but that's okay, because when the wheels are done you'll start cleaning the frame. Start at the top of the bike and work down, finishing with the cassette and pedals. Then switch off the cleaner to save fuel and water and to prevent someone else from borrowing it while your back is turned.

If you are working with buckets, then ignore them for a moment while you clean the wheels. The fastest and most efficient way to do this is simply to spin the wheel between your thumb and forefinger and scrape the mud from the sidewalls. This method may not be as glamorous as spraying with a pressure washer, but it leaves the wheels surprisingly clean. There will still be some mud left in the tread of the tire, however. Then, with a sponge, start at the top of the bike and work down. The saddle, the bars, the brake levers, and the three main frame tubes can be done in a matter of seconds. I do the rest of the bike from behind with the rear wheel supported between my knees. The pedals are next and can be done with a brush, if necessary.

Then comes the most important part—the transmission. Spin the pedals backward, and with your spoke or thin screwdriver clean the sprockets and between the chainrings. As you spin the pedals backward, use your fingers to clean the jockey wheels on the gear mechanism; this crud will be deposited onto the chain, so quickly give it a wipe too. Sponge off the remainder with a lot of water, and the bike should be relatively clean, except for the tire tread. Cleaning tires properly from a bucket takes time and too much water, so as long as the sidewalls are clean and the wheels spin freely, don't stress about having perfectly clean treads.

Whichever method you have used, get back into the pit front line so you can catch up with the state of play in the race. While waiting for your rider, dry the bike with your dry cloth, especially the saddle, the handlebars, and the frame tubes. Spray-lube the chain, jockey wheels, and front and rear derailleurs, and the bike should be ready to hand back. If you have any more time to spare before your rider appears, give the bike a once-over. Spin the wheels to check that they are straight and not catching the brakes, shift through the gears, and check to see that the bars and brake levers were not knocked askew on the course or when the bike was dropped. When you are satisfied it is all okay, get the bike in the correct gear, with the pedals set up as described above.

If time or water is short, you must do as much as you can to make the bike as efficient as possible. The main areas that clog up are the wheels, the pedals, the brakes, the sprockets, and the bottom-bracket area. Start with the wheels. With insufficient water you are fighting a losing battle trying to scrub them with a brush, so get your big screwdriver, hold it next to the tire sidewall, and spin the wheel, scraping the worst off. Use your spoke or thin screwdriver to clear the sprockets and chainrings, and use your fingers on the jockey wheels. If the transmission is free of mud and has a spray of oil, it will work fine. Poke out mud from the pedals, brakes, and bracket, in that order, and then spend time cleaning the bars and brake levers.

This may sound strange, but when a rider jumps on his bike, all he will see are his bars and front wheel, and he will feel whether the transmission is smooth. The rest of the bike can still be covered in mud, but he will not know it. He'll think the whole bike is clean and concentrate on the race, and he won't have to waste any mental effort thinking about how bad the bike feels and wishing he could get a decent mechanic!

Other Duties

You are not only a mechanic during a race; you must also fill the role of coach, manager, and adviser. You will probably need to be at both the starting line and the finish line to take warm-up clothing, provide a last-minute bottle of water or sports drink, or hand up the glasses your rider left in the car. At the finish, some warm clothing and words of congratulation should be pretty much it until your rider has cooled down, cleaned up, and changed. Try not to stand around listening to your rider's story of the race as she gets cold. Instead, remind her of the importance of getting warm and dry; you can hear the full account of the race later. If it's a UCI race, check the numbers of the riders selected for medical control (the list will be posted close to the finish line), and let your rider know immediately whether she is needed, as she will only have 30 minutes to report to the antidoping officer.

When you arrive at the venue and your rider is sorting himself out, take a walk around the circuit. Watch any preceding races and the other riders warming up. Make mental notes of the lines they are taking, whether certain sections are a ride or a run, and which areas might be congested on the early laps. Your rider will certainly do the same, but nerves soon get a grip and in some athletes this has an effect on rational thinking. Your rider may want to know what you think about a line, a tire choice, or the best tire pressure for the course, and if he does ask, you should be able to offer an informed opinion.

Once the race is under way, some riders like to get quick updates about the race at bike-changing time. Your rider may want to know her position, how much of a time gap she has in front and behind, and the general state of the race—whether she is losing time on the leaders, for example, and how much of the race is left. Although most riders do appreciate general words of encouragement, solid information offered at the same time—a clear time check, for example—can be even more helpful. After the initial laps have passed and the race has sorted itself out, try to keep your rider informed about two times: the gap to the rider in front (or behind, if your rider is leading) and how much of the race there is to go, as sometimes lap boards aren't easy to pick out in the heat of battle. Offer advice if you see that your rider is taking a wrong line or trying to ride something that other people are running faster. She might not take your advice, but it's better to be told than never to know.

Train your rider to communicate as clearly as possible with you during the bike change about any mechanical problems affecting the bike—that is, if anything other than a simple cleaning is needed. Punctures are pretty obvious, even to the most unmechanical person, but it is not very helpful when a rider throws his bike down screaming that it simply doesn't work. He should learn to tell you something that will make it easier to pinpoint the fault and make a quick repair. There are only seconds to get the information across, but "Brake problem" or "Gearing problem" is a lot better than no information at all.

Cyclocross racers rely on their helpers for support much more than other types of racers do in other cycling disciplines, and for the helpers it is very hard work. Having both ridden and helped as a mechanic, I am still of two minds about which is the harder job, especially when it comes to muddy races. I have certainly ended up just as dirty as a mechanic as I have as a racer. But as with other supporting roles, when you do the pit-crew job well, it is good to know you have contributed as part of a team to bringing about a success.

CHAPTER 8

Looking after Yourself

Looking after yourself and staying healthy are vital if you are to steer clear of injury and illness. Getting sick for a couple of weeks, or over-working yourself and pulling a muscle, can ruin part, or all, of a season. You are training hard and racing at a time of year when, to be honest, you really shouldn't be putting yourself under those kinds of stresses. Lack of sunlight and colder temperatures don't foster training adaptation, and it's the season for the general population to start sniffling. Hard training can lower your resistance, stress your immune system, and make you more susceptible to minor viral illnesses such as coughs and colds. A super-fit athlete is constantly treading a tightrope between being in top form and being ill.

You cannot pick up a cold virus from being cold and wet, but you can pick up one more easily when your resistance is lowered, and getting cold and wet stresses your system as your body fights to keep warm and stay healthy. Commonsense measures—washing your hands regularly, changing out of training clothes as soon as you get back into the house, dressing correctly while training, getting warm clothes on as soon as you finish a race, drying your hair after showering at the race—will help to reduce your chances of catching something.

Most viruses thrive in places where a lot of people congregate, typically in air-conditioned buildings and other places with relatively little fresh air, such as offices, bars, concerts and sporting events, vehicles for public transportation, and airplanes and airports. Your chances of catching a virus are higher in all these places, so if you can't avoid them, try to reduce your chances of being on the receiving end of those nasty airborne germs. Most of the transmission is either via the hand—from door handles, banisters, and anything else that a lot of people grab hold of—or in the air from sneezes and coughs. Regular hand-washing is an easy way to reduce the chances of these germs getting to you, but try to avoid touching your eyes or mouth as well.

Taking care of yourself is a bit like taking care of your bike. If you take care of your bike, it will look clean and shiny; you'll be more likely to spot problems with it right away, and it will look better and work more smoothly than if you neglected it. Likewise, if you are taking good care of yourself, you will look your best. Keep yourself clean, smart, and tidy. If you are looking good, you will feel better about yourself and make a better impression on others. If you are sponsored, either individually or as part of a team, you owe it to your sponsors and teammates to look your best at all times.

Moreover, just as your bike needs regular maintenance, you need to make sure you get regular medical checkups and that you get whatever medical tests are recommended for your gender and age group. Before the season starts, sort out any health problems you may have while you still have time. It is too easy to put things off once the season is under way. Make sure your visits to the dentist are up-to-date, that you have an annual physical exam, and that your tetanus shots are current. When riding 'cross, you will suffer more than your fair share of cuts and bruises, so take precautions to ensure they do not develop into anything more serious.

You shouldn't train in the same clothing more than once without washing it, especially when it comes to shorts and base layers. Bacterial skin complaints, especially on your point of contact with the saddle, thrive on sweat; if they are allowed to develop, antibiotics may be required to clear them up.

Eyes take a hammering in 'cross, too, because they are constantly subjected to mud, grit, and water. Follow the recommendations for eyewear mentioned in Chapter 2. Wash your eyes carefully after a race; if there is any inflammation, use an eye bath.

By taking time to look after yourself, you can save yourself from having to miss races or training due to an illness that could have been prevented. It takes much longer to get rid of a cold and its aftereffects than it does to prevent it in the first place.

As your cycling career progresses, you will be able to interpret what your body is telling you—whether you are doing too much, for example, or have an illness coming on. If you notice signs of an illness early and take steps to fight it, such as getting extra rest, drinking lots of fluids, and eating well, you will have a far better chance of recovering quickly and getting back into your training routine than if you just ignore it or continue to push yourself.

Colds and Viral Illnesses

Nobody is immune to colds and viruses, and no matter how careful you are, chances are you will suffer from them on occasion. If you're lucky, it will happen during the off-season and not a few days before the national championships!

By keeping an eye on your resting heart rate, it is possible to catch a pending illness early and reduce its impact before the main symptoms appear. A higher-than-normal resting heart rate indicates that your immune system is stressed and you may need to back off for a few days. Get lots of rest, forgo training for a couple of days, stay warm indoors, and take plenty of fluids.

Most over-the-counter medications are for cold relief; they relieve the symptoms, but they do not kill the virus. In recent years some products have come onto the market claiming to stop colds dead in their tracks, reducing the time it takes to recover from them. Unlike most cold-relief products, these products have natural ingredients. The most popular are micro-gel nasal sprays that are based on plant extracts that target the area deep inside the nasal cavity where cold germs first take hold and multiply; the spray is supposed to work by trapping cold-causing germs and helping your body remove them naturally. These products may be worth a try. There may be different ingredients in them in different countries and in different markets, however, even under the same brand name, and while at the current time I am not aware of any that appear on the UCI's "banned" list, it is vital that you check out anything you take to make sure it conforms to your country's antidoping regulations. If in doubt, ask a doctor to take a look at the ingredients, and if you're still unsure, do not take it. It's always better to be safe than sorry. If the ingredients of a specific product check out, you can start to use the product when you first notice signs of a cold or in the early stages of one, before your cold has fully developed—ideally, hit it hard when you first wake up with that tickly throat, and continue to use it for two days after the symptoms subside.

You can also increase your intake of vitamin C and add a zinc supplement when you feel a cold coming on, though studies to determine whether vitamin C has any real impact have been inconclusive. There are two things clinically proven to reduce the effects of a cold: zinc and chicken soup. If you are achy, you may want to take 400 milligrams of an ibuprofen-based painkiller three times a day with food. If a cold does take hold and you end up full of mucus, then try not to reinfect yourself with your own virus. Blow your nose with disposable tissues that you can throw away after every use, rather than cotton handkerchiefs, and if you sneeze, sneeze into the crook of your elbow instead of your hand. As previously mentioned, keep your hands clean! Even when you get back on your bike, remember to wash your gloves after each ride, as you will invariably be wiping your face and nose with your gloved hands as you clear your head.

To relieve congestion, use a steam inhalation. To do this, you can simply fill a bowl with very hot water, put a towel over your head, and breathe deeply through your mouth and nose. Or you might want to purchase a vaporizer or humidifier to use in your bedroom at night. Carvol, Vicks, and Olbas all make medicated solutions designed for use in vaporizers to help break up congestion and relieve coughing; follow package directions to add a small amount to the water in your vaporizer. A few drops of the same on your pillow at night will also help you breathe more easily and get a good night's sleep.

Any cold or cough that produces deep yellow or green mucus may require a trip to the doctor, as it means a secondary infection might have started. If so, a course of antibiotics may be the only way to shift it. It's important to always complete the whole course of antibiotics that was prescribed for you, even if symptoms subside or disappear. Whenever you must take antibiotics, eat plenty of yogurt with live acidophilus cultures for a while or take a probiotic supplement to re-place the good bacteria in your stomach that the antibiotics will be killing off.

As far as training goes, if you have a temperature of over 100 degrees Fahrenheit (38 degrees Celsius) a headache, aching joints or muscles, general fatigue, or any other symptoms that make it difficult to exer-cise, then you must avoid exerting yourself. This is your body's way of communicating to you that you need some rest; pushing yourself too hard at this point will simply prolong the illness and can cause postvi-ral fatigue as well as more serious conditions such as myocarditis.

When your temperature is back under 100 degrees Fahrenheit (38 degrees Celsius) and your aches have gone away, then light riding, with a heart rate under 70 percent of your max HR, can actually be beneficial and speed up recovery. Keep it short and low-key, and gradually build up as you begin to feel normal again.

And finally, never confuse a cold with a flu. While most people can expect to suffer from a cold pretty regularly, you will probably only experience full-blown flu once or twice in your lifetime. If you aren't sure of the difference, take note—it was once nicely described to me as follows: "If you are in bed feeling really bad and someone drops a $50 bill on the floor at the foot of your bed, if you have a cold you will crawl out and pick it up; if you have the flu, you will just roll over and go back to sleep!" If you think you have the flu, consult your physician to make sure you are doing everything you can to get better quickly.

Injuries

From time to time, you may be injured in a crash. Or you may develop sprains, strains, and twinges simply through working too hard. It is important to try to get these complaints sorted out quickly, before they develop into something more serious. By warming up thoroughly and stretching regularly, a lot of injuries can be prevented; the traumatic ones caused by falls cannot, but you must get appropriate medical care for them when they occur to ensure proper healing.

The standard treatment for an initial sprain or strain is RICE—rest, ice, compression, elevation. This therapy helps to reduce the swelling and restrict the spread of bruising, both of which can slow down the healing process. As soon as possible after an injury of this type, apply ice and a bandage and raise the affected part. If you are unsure how to apply the bandage correctly, get some expert help. You can also take an over-the-counter pain reliever. The first six hours after an injury are the most important, so act quickly. Never apply heat to a recent injury.

If pain or swelling increases, or you think the problem may be something more serious, such as a torn ligament, a dislocation, or a fracture, seek immediate medical treatment. If after your RICE treatment, the area still gives you problems, seek the help and guidance of a physical therapist, ideally one who has a background or interest in sports therapy. He or she will be able to diagnose the problem and recommend a program of treatment and exercises. Follow the physical therapist's directions and do the exercises; he or she knows far better than you do how long things take to mend and how to get back to full fitness in the shortest possible time. If you go out and train too soon, you may reinjure yourself.

Resume with light training when you can, but be careful not to overdo it. Gradually build up to the level you were at before. If you have any discomfort from the site of the injury, make sure it is simply because your muscles are working again after a layoff and not because you are working too hard or have had an insufficient recovery.

Massage

If you can get regular massage, then by all means take advantage of it, especially if hard training is making you tight and sore the following day. However, do not use massage as a substitute for your regular stretching. Massage can help reduce stiffness in an overworked muscle, but stretching is necessary to develop strong, flexible muscles and prevent injury. Self-massage is well worth the effort, as you can do it anywhere, you don't need anyone else's help, and it's less expensive to boot.

To give yourself a good massage, start in a sitting position—in the bathtub is ideal—begin at your ankle, and work up. First will be your calf muscles. Use steady stroking movements upward with gentle, firm pressure. Then move to the hamstrings at the back of the thigh, working in a similar way, and finish with the quadriceps at the front.

If you do your massage in the bathtub, the water and soap will reduce friction; otherwise, light oil is ideal. But do not use so much that you cannot grip, and never use any heat-generating massage creams.

Nutrition

Food provides the fuel you need to run your body. No matter how hard you train, how shiny your bikes are, or how great your determination is, if you don't provide your "engine" with the correct amount of the best-quality fuel, there is no way you can perform at your best.

The food you eat contains the following nutrients: carbohydrates, fats, and protein. It also contains vitamins, minerals, trace elements, dietary fiber, and water. No one food contains enough of each of these to meet the needs of the body fully; hence the need for a "balanced diet." The standard Western diet ensures that you get adequate supplies of all of the above—and in the case of fats, usually too much. However, you are not a standard Western person—you are a cyclist, and you need a bit more of certain things to cope with the raised levels of energy you have to produce.

The most important nutrients for you as a cyclist are the carbohydrates, particularly the complex carbs contained in foods such as potatoes, bread, pasta, rice, legumes, vegetables, and nuts. In addition to the starch within these foods, there are all the vitamins and minerals that are necessary to metabolize the carbohydrates. Simple carbs are usually found in highly processed foods in which the carbohydrate has been extracted from natural sources and broken down. Confectionary and sweet foods and drinks are usually high in simple carbs and contain "empty calories"—energy, but nothing else.

Fat is used as the "low-octane" fuel when riding. You need sufficient fat as a fuel source, especially on long rides, but as the traditional Western diet is too high in fat already, try to consume as little fatty food as possible. Your body will get all it needs from hidden fats in other foods.

Protein, as well as being required to manufacture and repair muscle, is another source of energy. The best sources of protein are white meats, fish, beans, legumes, vegetables, nuts, and low-fat milk.

Most people, especially athletes, are more aware of what they eat now than their predecessors were just a few years ago. The basic guidelines for a healthy diet are now widely known. Keep your intake of fat and sugar low; make sure your intake of complex carbohydrates is adequate; and eat as many fresh, raw, unrefined vegetables and fruits as possible. Adjust your calorie intake to your training schedule for adequate energy and recovery; on a heavy training day, you will need to take in more energy and nutrients than on a light training day, and during a rest week you can cut back a little on calories.

Reliance on junk food and fast food is unwise; it's usually the result of bad preparation or time management, ignorance, or just plain laziness. It only takes a couple of minutes longer to cook a bowl of fresh pasta than it does to microwave a "ready meal," and with some simple organization and well-planned shopping and cooking, you can have a nutritionally well-balanced and tasty meal sorted out well in advance. You won't have to eat junk food after a training ride if you have healthy foods with you; soon you may find you no longer crave them.

Breakfast is easy: Try muesli or a whole-grain cereal (avoid the kids' cereal shelf in the supermarket—anything that contains colors like that cannot be good for you!), or oatmeal or porridge. These choices can be made more interesting with the addition of chopped fruit, berries, nuts, and/or honey. Whole-grain toast, yogurt, and fresh orange juice are all quick, cheap, and full of the right stuff to fuel your morning and usually your main training session. At lunch or after morning training, a sandwich made from whole-grain bread and a low-fat but protein-rich filling, such as tuna or ham salad, is a quick and nutritious option. Pair this with fruit to round it out. In the evening, some combination of pasta or rice, baked or boiled potatoes, fresh vegetables or salad, and white meat or fish is again quick and easy. None of these choices present a culinary nightmare for even the worst chef to prepare! Keep it simple, and unless absolutely necessary, avoid any highly processed, prepared foods or foods in packages that have a list of ingredients on the side resembling a page from a chemistry textbook.

Post-training refueling is the most important part of your nutritional day: As mentioned in Chapter 6, you need to refuel with around 10 to 20 grams of protein and 30 to 50 grams of carbohydrate as soon as possible after a session. For a quick, easy strategy that gets the fuel back in where and when it's needed, simply make a recovery drink before you go out training and leave it in the fridge (try SiS ReGo or a similar commercial brand, or a homemade banana smoothie). If you drink this as soon as you get home, while you are getting showered and dressed, it should eliminate the immediate urge to eat sugary snacks and start the refueling process. Then you can take your time preparing a regular meal.

Between meals, snack on fresh fruit, muesli or granola bars, rice cakes, or nuts and dried fruit, and replace soft drinks, tea, and coffee with plain water or fresh fruit juice. And finally, don't worry about the occasional lapses—the odd burger or hot dog is not going to do you any long-term damage or ruin your season. Just don't rely on them every day.

As far as on-the-bike fueling goes, the bike-shop shelves are full nowadays of an assortment of brands of drinks, bars, and carbohydrate gels you can use on the bike. Regular use of these products will help keep you from underfueling your training effort—a common mistake. Work on consuming around 0.5 to 1.0 gram of carbohydrate per kilogram of body weight for each hour that you are out riding. for a rider who weighs 70 kilograms (154 lbs.), for example, that would be 35 to 70 grams per hour.

If you use a quality energy drink made with a maltodextrin glucose polymer, which is typically 98 percent carbohydrate, you can make a 4 to 7 percent solution in a 500-milliliter bottle that will give you enough carbs to fuel an hour or two of training. The solution strength will depend on the flavor and how strong a mix you can tolerate, but if you supplement the energy drink with bars (a good one will have around 40 grams of carbs) or gels (20 grams), you can always ensure you are taking in enough energy. In cold weather, it can be difficult to drink enough fluids; of course, you'll need to make sure you are getting enough fluids to replace your sweat loss and avoid dehydration, but bars and gels, followed by a gulp of water, can nevertheless be more appetizing than a sports drink at these times. Bars and gels also come in handy if you prefer a weaker mix of your favorite drink than is recommended in the package directions. Sports drinks can be too strong for either the palate or the stomach. Don't forget that a daily diet of glucose polymer drinks, bars, and gels can play havoc with your teeth, so keep them clean and don't miss your checkups.

Water

Water is probably the most important nutrient required by the body. It performs numerous essential functions, including temperature regulation during exercise. Water also acts as a transport medium, ferrying nutrients, wastes, and hormones around the body to and from various tissues.

Water losses through sweating can seriously affect performance, even at a rate of as little as 2 to 3 percent of body weight, so it is vital to keep hydrated at all times, especially after hard training. Always have a bottle at hand, whether in the house, at your office, on your bike, or traveling, and try to drink a minimum of 2 liters of plain water throughout the day, especially with meals.

CHAPTER 9

Cyclocross International

The past decade in the world of men's 'cross has been all about one nation: Belgium. Under the direction of the great seven-time world champion Eric De Vlaeminck, the Belgians started the drive in the mid-1990s. De Vlaeminck's focus and expertise were concentrated at that time on the younger age groups, and two names in particular: Sven Nys and Bart Wellens.

Nys popped up first at a Junior Worlds back in 1993, where he finished just outside of the top twenty, but a year later, in the sand at Koksijde on the Belgian coast, he just missed a medal, finishing fourth. By the time Nys was in his twenties, De Vlaeminck's work was paying dividends. The Nys-Wellens 1–2 at the U23 Worlds in 1997 and 1998 was a sign of things to come for the boys from Baal and Vorselaar, respectively, villages just 30 kilometers apart in a region northeast of Brussels. As the years have ticked by in the new millennium, Nys has proven to be the dominant rider of his generation and the man to beat. Although his record during any given season is formidable, however, his experiences at World Championships have been pretty miserable, with the exception of 2005 at St. Wendel, when he took the Elite crown for the first time.

Trying to hold form for an entire season—in which he has typically won a race almost every week from early September through January—seems to be a challenge for Nys. Or perhaps his troubles at the Worlds are simply due to the realities of dealing with the stress of the biggest 'cross day of the year. Regardless of the reason for his less-than-stellar showings, Nys needs to add to his rainbow jersey collection if he is to be held in the same esteem as his compatriots with five or more World wins to their name, such as Eric De Vlaeminck and Roland Liboton, or the Swiss Albert Zweifel. Nevertheless, Nys's 212 career wins to date, his domination of the season-long GVA and Super Prestige competitions, and his continued number-one position in the world rankings give him every right to be classed among the "greats" of the sport.

Actually, what Nys needs is some of the big-day coolness of his compatriot Erwin Vervecken. Nys knocks out twenty-plus wins every winter, whereas Vervecken is content with three or four, but come the third weekend in January, Vervecken is the guy who can handle the pressure cauldron. Out of eighteen appearances at World Championships, Vervecken has finished in the top six in twelve of them. He has been on the podium eight times, and three of those times he was on the very top step. Not too bad for someone who has not even been able to win the Belgian National Championships!

Nys and his rival Bart Wellens are on opposite ends of the scale, personality-wise. Nys is quiet and reserved; Wellens, who has the bigger fan base in Belgium, speaks his mind and always fights to the end. This became especially clear after his heartbreaking crash on the opening lap at the 2007 Worlds on his home ground in Flanders. The setback relegated him to the twenties, but his determined charge took him back through the field to an eventual fourth place. He never stopped trying, whereas Nys, caught up in the same opening lap crash (caused by a course marker that had been flicked into the path of the Belgian duo by a television-camera quad bike), lost heart and rolled in eleventh. Wellens had fractured his wrist in that crash and rode the remaining 61 minutes in a sea of pain as he tried to get back into the medals. Now that's the kind of fighter the Belgian person in the street likes!

But if you are looking for the next Belgian superstar, then you could do worse than put money on 20-year-old Niels Albert, the junior world champ from 2004 who won his first major Elite race against all the favorites at Loenhout over Christmas 2006. Unfortunately, his archrival is the super-talent Lars Boom from Holland, who made Niels Albert actually appear pretty ordinary as he, too, added to a junior title won in 2003 with a runaway win in the U23 title race at Hooglede-Gits. Boom is different from the Belgians in that he also races the road competitively for Rabobank, rather than just for preparation. It will be interesting to see which discipline he decides to focus on in the future.

Of the rest, it would be harsh to sum up a chapter in 'cross history without reference to Richard Groenendaal. Eleventh at his first junior Worlds in 1988 and winner the following year, he has been at the top of his profession every year since. He is one of only two riders who have been with super-squad Rabobank since it formed, which is a sign of his stature in Holland, although he recently announced he will ride out the last two years of his career with a new sponsor. At one point at the 2007 Worlds it looked as though he might add to the 2000 title that he won in his hometown of St. Michielsgestel. But a couple of ill-timed crashes put paid to that notion and he finished sixth—still not bad after twenty years of racing the Worlds.

On the women's racing scene, two names have dominated the Worlds results since the inception of the women's competition in 2000: Hanka Kupfernagel from Germany and Daphny Van Den Brand from Holland. Kupfernagel was the world number-one roadie during the late 1990s, topping the UCI ranking and culminating her road career with a silver medal in the road race at the Sydney

Olympics. Since she switched to racing on the dirt, her performances at the World Championships have been exceptional: She's won three gold medals, three silvers, and one bronze, and also came in fifth place one year. Van Den Brand has been almost as consistent, but not quite on Kupfernagel's level, with just the one win and four bronze medals, plus a fourth place, a sixth place, and an eleventh place.

Although the field sizes have only been increasing slowly, with forty to forty-five starters for the World Championships now the norm, women's racing has come of age. The quality and depth of competition among the women have increased dramatically, and there are now a number of 'cross specialists who, like the men, use the summer only as preparation and can make a living racing during the winter. The sideshow from 2000 has turned into the main act over the past couple of years, with an athleticism and a quality of racing that match the men's for excitement and spectacle. The chauvinist European crowds who simply used to turn up after lunch to watch the guys have now realized that they were missing something special.

The next nation to battle for World honors could be America. I've always suspected that my fellow Brits could never quite prop up the back of a Worlds field, as the Americans would always be just behind us. Great Britain is only a small 'cross nation, and we have only really had Roger Hammond to give us any real 'cross credibility. We have been just about far enough in front to be able to hide from the ridicule of the crowds, who up to this point have tended to focus their beer-fueled taunts on the Yanks with the long black socks, riding the bikes with the weird names so rarely seen in Europe, some of whom—get this—have beards! Add in a few competitors from Japan or Ukraine, and recently those crowd-pleasers from Zimbabwe, and there you have it.

But while Britain has stayed put down near the back, the United States has moved on significantly since the days of Paul Curley, Clark Natwick, Don Myrah, and Dave McLaughlin, and a medal trickle that started in 1999 turned into a relative deluge in 2007. It's Matt Kelly's fault; he started it all, winning a junior gold medal in the snow at Poprad, Slovakia, and to prove it was no fluke, Will Frischkorn backed him up pretty well in fifth place. Later that very same day, Tim Johnson finished third in the U23 race behind a dominant Wellens, who came in first, and his compatriot Tom Vannoppen, who just managed to outsprint Johnson. The following year, Walker Ferguson, a World junior and U23 mountain-bike medalist, proved it was no one-year flash in the pan as he finished in the silver-medal spot at St. Michielsgestel in Holland. This was starting to get serious, but as the guys who beat Kelly (Sven Vanthourenhout) and Ferguson (Bart Aernouts) moved on to greater things with Rabobank, so the American boys faded away, never to be seen again on the big 'cross scene in Europe. They have both made comebacks with various degrees of success on mountain bikes in the States, however, in the past couple of years.

Tim Johnson also went missing for a while (though he came back strongly in Elite domestic competition in 2006), and so it was left to the American women to figure strongly in the Worlds for a while. Alison Dunlap came close to a medal in 2002, with fourth place at Zolder, Belgium, losing out in a three-up sprint for silver. Add to this her two fifth places and the fourth-place finishes of the two Anns, Ann Grande and Ann Knapp, and that is as close as the Americans got until 2007. This is the year the spree of silvers started with a spirited sprint by Danny Summerhill in the junior race, matched the next day by Katie Compton, who only lost out to teamwork by two French women. Then, Jonathan Page was outdone only by the vastly more experienced Erwin Vervecken, who was nevertheless probably weaker that day. This despite the fact that Page's season had been devastated by a shoulder injury that he picked up in a training crash at the opening World Cup of the season.

What are the odds of an American winning a rainbow jersey in the next decade, perhaps even on American soil? I'll keep my wallet firmly in my pocket!

With a career that started with a junior world title in 1989, Dutchman Richard Groenendaal was still a man to beat twenty years later, as he showed at the 2007 championships, where he led for much of the race.

The United States has led the way in attracting large participation in women's 'cross racing, and the large pool has delivered consistent top-10 finishers at the World Championships every year.

World Championships Results, 1997–2007

MUNICH, GERMANY, 1997

Juniors

1. David Rusch	Switzerland	46.14
2. Stefano Toffoletti	Italy	@0.05
3. Steffen Weigold	Germany	@0.06
4. Nicolas Dieudonne	France	@0.08
5. Torsten Hieckmann	Germany	@0.11
6. John Gadret	France	@0.12
7. Thomas Lecuyer	France	@0.25
8. Andrew Vancoillie	Belgium	@1.14
9. Davy Commeyne	Belgium	@1.22
10. Wilant Van Gils	Netherlands	@1.30

U23

1. Sven Nys	Belgium	53.25
2. Bart Wellens	Belgium	@ same time (s.t.)
3. Christophe Morel	France	@0.22
4. Miguel Martinez	France	@0.38
5. Gretenius Gommers	Netherlands	@0.58
6. Elvis Zucchi	Italy	@1.33
7. Guillaume Benoist	France	@1.37
8. Gerben De Knegt	Netherlands	@1.45
9. Zdenek Mlynar	Czech Republic	@1.46
10. David Willemsens	Belgium	@1.47

Elite

1. Daniele Pontoni	Italy	1.00.40
2. Thomas Frischknecht	Switzerland	@0.23
3. Luca Bramati	Italy	@0.23
4. Adri Van Der Poel	Netherlands	@0.35
5. Wim De Vos	Netherlands	@0.53
6. Erwin Vervecken	Belgium	@1.13
7. Franz-Josef Nieberding	Germany	@1.25
8. Beat Wabel	Switzerland	@1.39
9. Dieter Runkel	Switzerland	@1.39
10. Peter Van Santvliet	Belgium	@2.04

MIDDELFART, DENMARK, 1998

Juniors

1. Michael Baumgartner	Switzerland	38.56

2. Stefano Toffoletti	Italy	@0.03
3. Davy Commeyne	Belgium	@s.t.
4. Martin Ocasek	Czech Republic	@0.05
5. Sven Vanthourenhout	Belgium	@0.09
6. Bjorn Schroder	Germany	@s.t.
7. Tilo Schuler	Germany	@0.16
8. Tomas Trunschka	Czech Republic	@s.t.
9. Pavel Bartos	Czech Republic	@s.t.
10. Gregory Rast	Switzerland	@s.t.

U23

1. Sven Nys	Belgium	52.14
2. Bart Wellens	Belgium	@0.24
3. Petr Dlask	Czech Republic	@0.29
4. Klaus Nielson	Denmark	@0.45
5. Guillaume Benoist	France	@0.47
6. Pawel Prosek	Czech Republic	@0.59
7. Maarten Nijland	Netherlands	@1.08
8. Raymond Lubberman	Netherlands	@1.10
9. Fabrizio Dall'Oste	Italy	@1.12
10. Tim Johnson	USA	@s.t.

Elite

1. Mario De Clerq	Belgium	1.04.06
2. Erwin Vervecken	Belgium	@1.04
3. Henrik Djernis	Denmark	@1.07
4. Daniele Pontoni	Italy	@s.t.
5. Radomir Simunek	Czech Republic	@1.19
6. Emmanuel Magnien	France	@1.23
7. Dieter Runkel	Switzerland	@1.55
8. Christophe Mengin	France	@2.17
9. Richard Groenendaal	Netherlands	@2.28
10. Beat Wabel	Switzerland	@2.31

POPRAD, SLOVAKIA, 1999

Juniors

1. Matthew Kelly	USA	37.26
2. Sven Vanthourenhout	Belgium	@0.01
3. Thijs Verhagen	Netherlands	@0.12
4. David Kasek	Czech Republic	@1.04
5. William Frishkorn	USA	@1.07
6. Jean-Baptiste Beraud	France	@s.t.

7. Tim Van Nuffel	Netherlands	@1.22
8. Wouter Bunning	Netherlands	@1.28
9. Ronald Heigl	Switzerland	@1.35
10. Hannes Genze	Germany	@1.42

U23

1. Bart Wellens	Belgium	53.47
2. Tom Vannoppen	Belgium	@1.34
3. Tim Johnson	USA	@1.35
4. Steffen Weigold	Germany	@1.53
5. John Gadret	France	@2.05
6. Guillaume Benoist	France	@2.32
7. Emil Hekele	Czech Republic	@2.38
8. David Derepas	France	@2.40
9. David Sussemilch	Czech Republic	@2.51
10. Pascal Van Bussel	Netherlands	@3.06

Elite

1. Mario De Clerq	Belgium	1.02.50
2. Erwin Vervecken	Belgium	@0.08
3. Adri Van Der Poel	Netherlands	@0.24
4. Daniele Pontoni	Italy	@1.24
5. Thomas Frischknecht	Switzerland	@1.42
6. Sven Nys	Belgium	@2.09
7. Radomir Simunek	Czech Republic	@2.13
8. Peter Van Santvliet	Belgium	@2.49
9. Jiri Pospisil	Czech Republic	@3.17
10. Ben Berden	Belgium	@3.41

ST. MICHIELSGESTEL, NETHERLANDS, 2000

Juniors

1. Bart Aernouts	Belgium	41.06
2. Walker Ferguson	USA	@0.15
3. David Kasek	Czech Republic	@0.47
4. Kenny Van Hummel	Netherlands	@s.t.
5. Pieter Ghyllbert	Belgium	@s.t.
6. Koen De Kort	Netherlands	@s.t.
7. Vladimir Kyziuat	Czech Republic	@0.50
8. Sven Haussler	Germany	@s.t.
9. Enrico Franzoi	Italy	@0.51
10. Klaas Vantornout	Belgium	@0.52

U23

1. Bart Wellens	Belgium	53.32
2. Tom Vannoppen	Belgium	@0.44
3. Davy Commeyne	Belgium	@1.04
4. David Derepas	France	@1.36
5. Camiel Van Den Bergh	Netherlands	@1.38
6. Steffen Weigold	Germany	@1.39
7. Sven Vanthourenhout	Belgium	@s.t.
8. Wilant Van Gils	Netherlands	@2.15
9. Thijs Volker	Netherlands	@2.24
10. Roel Van Houtum	Netherlands	@2.29

Women

1. Hanka Kupfernagel	Germany	42.10
2. Louise Robinson	Great Britain	@0.57
3. Daphny Van Den Brand	Netherlands	@1.16
4. Laurence Leboucher	France	@2.03
5. Alison Dunlap	USA	@2.30
6. Corine Dorland	Netherlands	@2.55
7. Alla Epifanova	Russia	@3.14
8. Carmen Richardson	USA	@3.15
9. Inge Velthuis	Netherlands	@3.36
10. Chantal Daucourt	Switzerland	@3.57

Elite

1. Richard Groenendaal	Netherlands	59.57
2. Mario De Clerq	Belgium	@0.38
3. Sven Nys	Belgium	@0.42
4. Adrie Van Der Poel	Netherlands	@1.18
5. Wim De Vos	Netherlands	@1.50
6. Ben Berden	Belgium	@2.08
7. Peter Van Santvliet	Belgium	@2.12
8. Gerben De Knegt	Netherlands	@2.17
9. Daniele Pontoni	Italy	@2.22
10. Dominique Arnould	France	@2.23

TABOR, CZECH REPUBLIC, 2001

Juniors

1. Martin Bina	Czech Republic	38.54
2. Radomir Simunek	Czech Republic	@0.19
3. Jan Kunta	Czech Republic	@s.t.
4. Romain Fondard	France	@0.40

5. Pascal Vaillant	France	@s.t.
6. Milan Vocadlo	Czech Republic	@s.t.
7. Geert Wellens	Belgium	@0.56
8. Mariusz Gil	Poland	@1.06
9. Kor Steenbergen	Netherlands	@1.18
10. Simon Zahner	Switzerland	@1.21

U23

1. Sven Vanthourenhout	Belgium	51.55
2. Tomas Trunschka	Czech Republic	@0.16
3. David Kasek	Czech Republic	@0.36
4. Wim Jacobs	Belgium	@0.38
5. Aurelien Clerc	Switzerland	@0.40
6. Wilant Van Gils	Netherlands	@0.43
7. Martin Zlamalik	Czech Republic	@0.53
8. Davy Commeyne	Belgium	@s.t.
9. Josef Soukup	Czech Republic	@s.t.
10. Freek De Jonge	Netherlands	@s.t.

Women

1. Hanka Kupfernagel	Germany	28.29
2. Corine Dorland	Netherlands	@0.35
3. Daphny Van Den Brand	Netherlands	@0.41
4. Ann Grande	USA	@0.45
5. Laurence Leboucher	France	@0.47
6. Louise Robinson	Great Britain	@1.02
7. Nicole Cooke	Great Britain	@1.06
8. Debby Mansfield	Netherlands	@1.08
9. Rachel Lloyd	USA	@1.18
10. Reza Hormes-Ravenstijn	Netherlands	@2.05

Elite

1. Erwin Vervecken	Belgium	1.01.54
2. Petr Dlask	Czech Republic	@0.01
3. Mario De Clerq	Belgium	@0.14
4. Sven Nys	Belgium	@1.07
5. Jiri Pospisil	Czech Republic	@1.11
6. Henrik Djernis	Denmark	@1.29
7. Gerben De Knegt	Netherlands	@1.41
8. Camiel Van Den Bergh	Netherlands	@1.49
9. Tom Vannoppen	Belgium	@2.25
10. Vaclav Jezek	Czech Republic	@2.36

ZOLDER, BELGIUM, 2002

Juniors
1. Kevin Pauwels	Belgium	43.41
2. Krysztof Kuzniak	Poland	@0.11
3. Zdenek Stybar	Czech Republic	@0.15
4. Jaroslav Kulhavy	Czech Republic	@0.26
5. Mike Thielemans	Belgium	@0.34
6. Felix Gniot	Germany	@s.t.
7. Derik Zampedri	Italy	@s.t.
8. Jens Petroll	Germany	@0.37
9. Dieter Vanthourenhout	Belgium	@0.44
10. Pirmin Lan	Switzerland	@0.56

U23
1. Thijs Verhagen	Netherlands	49.48
2. Davy Commeyne	Belgium	@s.t.
3. Tomas Trunschka	Czech Republic	@s.t.
4. Enrico Franzoi	Italy	@s.t.
5. Wim Jacobs	Belgium	@s.t.
6. Martin Bina	Czech Republic	@0.37
7. Michael Baumgartner	Switzerland	@0.53
8. Adam Craig	USA	@1.12
9. Radomir Simunek	Czech Republic	@1.36
10. Steve Chainel	France	@1.44

Women
1. Laurence Leboucher	France	39.06
2. Hanka Kupfernagel	Germany	@1.04
3. Daphny Van Den Brand	Netherlands	@s.t.
4. Alison Dunlap	USA	@s.t.
5. Ann Grande	USA	@1.41
6. Anja Nobus	Belgium	@2.00
7. Reza Hormes-Ravenstijn	Netherlands	@s.t.
8. Birgit Hollmann	Germany	@s.t.
9. Hilde Quintens	Belgium	@2.05
10. Carmen D'Alusio	USA	@2.12

Elite
1. Mario De Clerq	Belgium	1.01.11
2. Tom Vannoppen	Belgium	@0.03
3. Sven Nys	Belgium	@0.06
4. Richard Groenendaal	Netherlands	@0.10
5. Gerben De Knegt	Netherlands	@0.14

6. Dominique Arnould	France	@0.21
7. Wim De Vos	Netherlands	@0.22
8. Bart Wellens	Belgium	@0.26
9. Ben Berden	Belgium	@1.19
10. Thomas Frischknecht	Switzerland	@1.38

MONOPOLI, ITALY, 2003

Juniors

1. Lars Boom	Netherlands	37.51
2. Eddy Van Ijzendoorn	Netherlands	@0.30
3. Zdenek Stybar	Czech Republic	@0.36
4. Sebastian Langeveld	Netherlands	@0.39
5. Romain Villa	France	@1.01
6. Jan Sel	Czech Republic	@1.07
7. Niels Albert	Belgium	@1.34
8. Frantisek Kloucek	Czech Republic	@1.38
9. Clement L'Hotellerie	France	@1.39
10. Tom Van Den Bosch	Belgium	@1.55

U23

1. Enrico Franzoi	Italy	49.22
2. Wesley Van Der Linden	Belgium	@0.28
3. Thijs Verhagen	Netherlands	@0.35
4. Martin Bina	Czech Republic	@1.25
5. Bart Aernouts	Belgium	@1.31
6. Jean-Baptiste Beraud	France	@1.32
7. Tim Van Nuffel	Belgium	@1.33
8. Steve Chainel	France	@1.35
9. Pieter Weening	Netherlands	@1.36
10. Theo Eltink	Netherlands	@s.t.

Women

1. Daphny Van Den Brand	Netherlands	38.24
2. Hanka Kupfernagel	Germany	@0.02
3. Laurence Leboucher	France	@0.16
4. Annabella Stropparo	Italy	@0.31
5. Mette Andersen	Denmark	@1.05
6. Maria Turcutto	Italy	@1.10
7. Marilyne Salvetat	France	@1.19
8. Nicolle De Bie-Leijten	Belgium	@1.23
9. Corine Dorland	Netherlands	@1.24
10. Ann Grande	USA	@s.t.

Elite

1. Bart Wellens	Belgium	56.43
2. Mario De Clerq	Belgium	@0.38
3. Erwin Vervecken	Belgium	@1.20
4. Ben Berden	Belgium	@1.28
5. Sven Nys	Belgium	@2.07
6. Francis Mourey	France	@s.t.
7. Daniele Pontoni	Italy	@s.t.
8. Tom Vannoppen	Belgium	@2.24
9. Jiri Pospisil	Czech Republic	@2.26
10. Arnauld Labbe	France	@s.t.

PONCHÂTEAU, FRANCE, 2004

Juniors

1. Niels Albert	Belgium	40.33
2. Roman Kreuziger	Czech Republic	@0.22
3. Clement L'Hotellerie	France	@1.29
4. Clement Cid	France	@1.47
5. Petr Novotny	Czech Republic	@1.49
6. Jan Skarnitzl	Czech Republic	@2.05
7. Rene Lang	Switzerland	@2.10
8. Thijs Van Amerongen	Netherlands	@2.44
9. Damien Robert	France	@2.46
10. Jonathan Lopez	France	@s.t.

U23

1. Kevin Pauwels	Belgium	49.38
2. Mariusz Gil	Poland	@0.08
3. Martin Zlamalik	Czech Republic	@0.16
4. Sebastien Minard	France	@s.t.
5. Lukas Fluckiger	Switzerland	@0.18
6. Zdenek Stybar	Czech Republic	@0.25
7. Krysztof Kuzniak	Poland	@s.t.
8. Enrico Franzoi	Italy	@s.t.
9. Klaas Vantornout	Belgium	@0.29
10. Wesley Van Der Linden	Belgium	@s.t.

Women

1. Laurence Leboucher	France	43.06
2. Maryline Salvetat	France	@0.37
3. Hanka Kupfernagel	Germany	@0.51
4. Ann Knapp	USA	@1.48
5. Alison Dunlap	USA	@1.54

6. Louise Robinson	Great Britain	@2.02
7. Marianne Vos	Netherlands	@2.40
8. Corinne Sempe	France	@2.43
9. Reza Hormes-Ravenstijn	Netherlands	@2.44
10. Birgit Hollmann	Germany	@2.46

Elite

1. Bart Wellens	Belgium	1.02.19
2. Mario De Clerq	Belgium	@s.t.
3. Sven Vanthourenhout	Belgium	@0.07
4. Daniele Pontoni	Italy	@0.21
5. Ben Berden	Belgium	@0.24
6. Erwin Vervecken	Belgium	@0.29
7. Francis Mourey	France	@0.38
8. Petr Dlask	Czech Republic	@0.40
9. Michael Baumgartner	Switzerland	@0.49
10. Alessandro Fontana	Italy	@1.09

ST. WENDEL, GERMANY, 2005

Juniors

1. Davide Malacarne	Italy	38.52
2. Julien Taramarcaz	Switzerland	@s.t.
3. Christoph Pfingsten	Germany	@s.t.
4. Romain Lejeune	France	@0.10
5. Ricardo Van Der Velde	Netherlands	@0.14
6. Lukas Kloucek	Czech Republic	@0.42
7. Ondrej Bambula	Czech Republic	@0.49
8. Yannick Martinez	France	@s.t.
9. Robert Gavenda	Slovakia	@0.50
10. Guillaume Perrot	France	@0.51

U23

1. Zdenek Stybar	Czech Republic	50.12
2. Radomir Simunek	Czech Republic	@0.21
3. Simon Zahner	Switzerland	@0.25
4. Lukas Fluckiger	Switzerland	@0.28
5. Niels Albert	Belgium	@0.35
6. Kevin Pauwels	Belgium	@0.59
7. Derik Zampedri	Italy	@1.25
8. Steve Chainel	France	@1.27
9. Lars Boom	Netherlands	@1.28
10. Krysztof Kuzniak	Poland	@s.t.

Women

1. Hanka Kupfernagel	Germany	41.42
2. Sabine Spitz	Germany	@0.28
3. Mirjam Melchers	Netherlands	@0.32
4. Laurence Leboucher	France	@s.t.
5. Maryline Salvetat	France	@s.t.
6. Daphny Van Den Brand	Netherlands	@2.02
7. Ann Knapp	USA	@2.16
8. Anja Nobus	Belgium	@2.24
9. Marianne Vos	Netherlands	@2.25
10. Nadia Triquet	France	@2.47

Elite

1. Sven Nys	Belgium	1.01.34
2. Erwin Vervecken	Belgium	@0.02
3. Sven Vanthourenhout	Belgium	@0.13
4. Francis Mourey	France	@0.31
5. Davy Commeyne	Belgium	@s.t.
6. Tom Vannoppen	Belgium	@s.t.
7. Petr Dlask	Czech Republic	@s.t.
8. Enrico Franzoi	Italy	@s.t.
9. Michael Baumgartner	Switzerland	@s.t.
10. Wilant Van Gils	Netherlands	@s.t.

ZEDDAM, NETHERLANDS, 2006

Juniors

1. Boy Van Poppel	Netherlands	38.03
2. Robert Gavenda	Slovakia	@0.03
3. Tom Meeusen	Belgium	@0.09
4. Yannick Martinez	France	@0.14
5. Sascha Weber	Germany	@0.20
6. David Menger	Czech Republic	@s.t.
7. Bjorn Selander	USA	@s.t.
8. Mathias Fluckiger	Switzerland	@0.37
9. Johim Ariensen	Netherlands	@0.38
10. Sylwester Janiszewski	Poland	@s.t.

U23

1. Zdenek Stybar	Czech Republic	51.01
2. Lars Boom	Netherlands	@s.t.
3. Niels Albert	Belgium	@s.t.
4. Aurelio Fontana	Italy	@1.03

5. Lukas Fluckiger	Switzerland	@1.08
6. Sebastian Langeveld	Netherlands	@1.25
7. Romain Villa	France	@1.31
8. Jempy Drucker	Luxembourg	@1.32
9. Dieter Vanthourenhout	Belgium	@1.37
10. Paul Voss	Germany	@1.38

Women

1. Marianne Vos	Netherlands	39.14
2. Hanka Kupfernagel	Germany	@s.t.
3. Daphny Van Den Brand	Netherlands	@0.52
4. Mirjam Melchers–Van Poppel	Netherlands	@1.16
5. Helen Wyman	Great Britain	@2.22
6. Maryline Salvetat	France	@2.26
7. Nadia Triquet-Claude	France	@2.29
8. Birgit Hollmann	Germany	@2.30
9. Ann Knapp	USA	@2.31
10. Lyne Bessette	Canada	@2.40

Elite

1. Erwin Vervecken	Belgium	1.05.40
2. Bart Wellens	Belgium	@0.02
3. Francis Mourey	France	@s.t.
4. Steve Chainel	France	@0.12
5. Tom Vannoppen	Belgium	@0.15
6. Kamil Ausbuher	Czech Republic	@0.19
7. Enrico Franzoi	Italy	@0.32
8. Gerben De Knegt	Netherlands	@0.46
9. Vladimir Kyzivat	Czech Republic	@0.49
10. Jonathan Page	USA	@0.50

HOOGLEDE-GITS, BELGIUM, 2007

Juniors

1. Joeri Adams	Belgium	41.18
2. Danny Summerhill	USA	@0.01
3. Jiri Polnicky	Czech Republic	@s.t.
4. Ramon Sinkeldam	Netherlands	@0.02
5. Ole Quast	Germany	@0.11
6. Arnaud Jouffroy	France	@0.32
7. Alesandro Calderan	Italy	@0.44
8. Rob Van Der Velde	Netherlands	@0.58
9. Marek Konwa	Poland	@1.06
10. Peter Sagan	Slovakia	@1.10

U23

1. Lars Boom	Netherlands	53.53
2. Niels Albert	Belgium	@1.22
3. Romain Villa	France	@1.44
4. Zdenek Stybar	Czech Republic	@2.29
5. Philipp Walsleben	Germany	@2.49
6. Lukas Kloucek	Czech Republic	@2.56
7. Jonathan Lopez	France	@3.04
8. Rob Peeters	Belgium	@3.10
9. Rafael Visinelli	Italy	@3.22
10. Ricardo Van Der Velde	Netherlands	@3.25

Women

1. Maryline Salvetat	France	42.51
2. Katie Compton	USA	@0.01
3. Laurence Leboucher	France	@0.09
4. Daphny Van Den Brand	Netherlands	@0.31
5. Hanka Kupfernagel	Germany	@0.41
6. Christel Ferrier-Bruneau	France	@0.43
7. Marianne Vos	Netherlands	@1.12
8. Birgit Hollmann	Germany	@1.33
9. Helen Wyman	Great Britain	@2.26
10. Linda Van Rijen	Netherlands	@2.42

Elite

1. Erwin Vervecken	Belgium	1.05.35
2. Jonathan Page	USA	@0.03
3. Enrico Franzoi	Italy	@0.16
4. Bart Wellens	Belgium	@0.25
5. Kevin Pauwels	Belgium	@0.32
6. Richard Groenendaal	Netherlands	@0.35
7. Gerben De Knegt	Netherlands	@1.12
8. John Gadret	France	@1.26
9. Christian Heule	Switzerland	@1.35
10. Thijs Al	Netherlands	@1.40

RECOMMENDED READING

BOOKS

Van de Gejuchte, D., and P. Sergent. *La gloire dans les Labours*. Editions Eecloonaar, 1996.

Friel, D., and W. Hobson. *Workouts in a Binder® for Indoor Cycling*. Boulder, CO: VeloPress, 2006.

The Cyclist's Training Diary. Boulder, CO: VeloPress, 2007.

WEB SITES

General Information and Country Cyclocross News

www.cyclo-cross.info—Belgian site with up-to-date results (*uitslagen*) and reports on all the central European races, in Flemish

www.new.cyclocrossonline.be/—As above, in Flemish

www.cyclocrossworld.com—American site with news, results, and shop and tech info and advice

www.radquer.ch—Swiss cyclocross news

www.superprestigecyclocross.com—Web site of the Euro race series

www.teamcyclocross44.free.fr—French cyclocross news

www.velonews.com—American site with cycling news

Web Sites of World Championship Racers

1. **Niels Albert**, www.nielsalbert.net
2. **Lars Boom**, www.larsboom.nl
3. **Gerben De Knegt**, http://www.gerbendeknegt.nl

4. **Enrico Franzoi**, www.enricofranzoi.tk

   Fan club membership mail, aramat@advalvas.be

5. **Richard Groenendaal**, www.richardgroenendaal.nl

6. **Christian Heule**, www.christian-heule.com

7. **Hanka Kupfernagel**, www.hanka-kupfernagel.de

8. **Sven Nys**, www.svennys.com

   Fan club membership mail, bestuur@svennys.com

9. **Jonathan Page**, www.thejonathanpage.com

10. **Zdenek Stybar**, www.zdenekstybar.com

    Fan club membership mail, supportersclub@zdenekstybar.com

11. **Ryan Trebon**, http://ryantrebon.blog.com

12. **Daphny Van Den Brand**, www.daphnyvandenbrand.nl

13. **Sven Vanthourenhout**, www.svenvanthourenhout.be

14. **Klaas Vantornout**, http://users.telenet.be/vantornoutklaas/home.htm

15. **Erwin Vervecken**, www.cyclocross.be

    Fan club membership mail, peter_van_echelpoel@belgacom.net

16. **Marianne Vos**, www.mariannevos.nl

17. **Bart Wellens**, www.bartwellens.be

    Fan club membership mail, supportersclub@bartwellens.be

18. **Helen Wyman**, www.helenwyman.com

INDEX

ABOUT THE AUTHOR

Simon Burney spent three years racing the professional cyclocross circuit before an injury forced him into team management. For the past twenty years Simon has been managing cyclocross and mountain bike teams. As a manager of professional teams through the 1990s, Simon was privileged to work with the finest 'cross riders of that generation: world champions Dominique Arnould and Henrik Djernis, plus Beat Wabel, and Peter Van Den Abeele, among others.

Simon served as manager of the Great Britain mountain bike team in the 2000 and 2004 Olympic Games. In the 2002 and 2006 Commonwealth Games, he was manager of the English team. Since 2000, Simon has worked for British Cycling as the performance manager of their mountain bike and cyclocross teams, and continues to manage the national team at the world championships.

The 2007 World Championships at Hooglede-Gits was Simon's twenty-sixth consecutive year at Worlds as either a rider, mechanic, team manager, or spectator, and he vows to keep going until an English speaker (preferably a Brit!) wins the elite race.